DAINTY
DESSERTS
FOR
DAINTY
PEOPLE

KNOX
GELATINE

TRADE MARK REG. U. S. PAT. OFF

KNOX
SPARKLING GRANULATED
GELATINE

Makes
Desserts, Salads,
Puddings, Sherbets,
Jellies, Ice Creams,
and Candies.

Published by

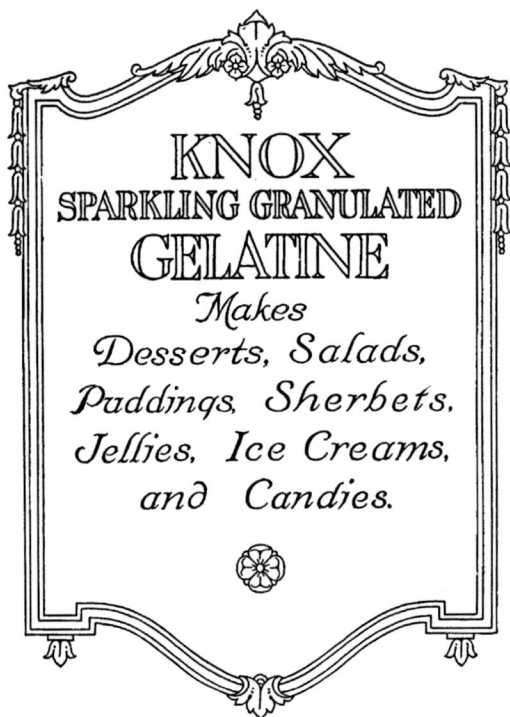

CHARLES B. KNOX COMPANY
INCORPORATED.
JOHNSTOWN, N.Y., U.S.A.

Printing Statement:

Due to the very old age and scarcity of this book,
many of the pages may be hard to read due to the
blurring of the original text, possible missing pages,
missing text, dark backgrounds and other issues
beyond our control.

Because this is such an important and rare work, we
believe it is best to reproduce this book regardless of
its original condition.

Thank you for your understanding.

Knox
Dainty Desserts
for
Dainty People

THERE is no part of the meal which demands more thought than the dessert. We are all content with the good old standbys for the principal courses, but with desserts It is different. Our hunger is partially satisfied by the time they appear, and we are in a more critical mood. We want something attractive to look at, and something that will gratify our sense of taste and not make too serious demands upon our digestion. The pies and hot puddings of our grandmother's days have waned in popularity, and in their places are to be found cold and frozen desserts. For the making of these new dishes gelatine is indispensable. It may be used in an almost endless variety of ways. It makes possible numberless dishes, not less delightful to the eye than pleasing to the palate, and opens the door to constantly new achievements in culinary inventions. And gelatine is not limited in Its use to the dessert course. It does service in the making of other savory dishes from soup to dessert. It is a boon in the preparation of every part of the meal.

Knox Sparkling Gelatine is made under the very best sanitary conditions and from the very best materials, and when it is made into jelly it produces that clear, sparkling effect which has made it so justly celebrated.

It is our hope that with the aid of this little book the housewife will find the making of a great variety of appetizing, nourishing and attractive dishes easier and more pleasant.

It must be remembered, however, that the recipes in this book are prepared for use with Knox Gelatine only, and to have good results no other gelatine can be used.

Knox Sparkling Gelatine is endorsed by the leading Pure Food Experts, and is used daily in homes and by domestic science teachers and teachers of cookery in the foremost cooking schools and hospital training classes in the United States and Canada, and the experience of these people has taught them to use none but the best.

Each package of Knox Sparkling Gelatine and Knox Acidulated Gelatine is sold under the positive GUARANTEE of money back if for any reason you are not satisfied.

Knox Sparkling Granulated Gelatine is put up in two packages. No. 1 is the Plain Sparkling (yellow package), and is the original, un-flavored, unsweetened gelatine. No. 3 is the Sparkling Acidulated (blue package). Both packages are alike, containing two envelopes of gelatine, and an envelope of Pink Vegetable Coloring for making a col-ored dessert, salad or icing for cake, and make the same quantity—TWO QUARTS of jelly. The only difference between the two packages is that the No. 3 Acidulated contains an envelope of Lemon Flavoring, which takes the place of lemon juice and affords a ready prepared flavoring. The flavoring and coloring are not mixed with the gelatine in either package, but packed in separate envelopes, thus leaving it to the purchasers to use them or not as they desire. With the No. 1 Plain package the natural fruit juices of lemons, oranges, etc., are used for flavoring, while with the No. 3 Acidulated (Busy Housekeeper's) pack-age the Lemon Flavoring is furnished in concentrated form ready for use. All that is added is water and sugar, and the jelly is ready to mold.

Housekeepers will have no trouble in measuring Knox Gelatine, as it is already measured in two envelopes, each one making one quart of jelly. This makes it very convenient when less than a full package is to be used, and being so divided it may be used in serving a small family as well as a large party.

Birthday Cake
(See Page 41)

QUANTITY OF LIQUID JELLIED BY A PACKAGE OF KNOX SPARKLING GELATINE

Each package of Knox Gelatine makes TWO QUARTS of jelly—FOUR TIMES as much as the ready prepared packages on the market that make but one pint. That is why Knox Gelatine is so economical.

In the summer, however, and especially if the dish is to be served within two hours after molding, it is advisable to decrease slightly the quantity of liquid. In making aspic jelly, for molding meat, fish, and salad, where heavy materials are to be held up, one package of **Knox** Sparkling Gelatine will be required for each five cups of liquid. Remember that a package (two envelopes) of **Knox** Sparkling Gelatine will jell two quarts of liquid, one-half package (one envelope) one quart, and one-fourth package (one-half envelope) one pint. In trying a new recipe, estimate the full quantity of liquid required by the recipe, and see that the quantity of gelatine is proportioned correctly.

TO MOLD AND UNMOLD GELATINE MIXTURES QUICKLY

By the use of crushed ice and rock salt, jelly made with **Knox** Gelatine may be molded at any season in one hour. When ice and salt are not at hand, set the dish containing the gelatine mixture in cold water, or in salt and water. In winter the mold may be packed in snow, or covered and set out of doors.

To unmold, immerse the mold to the top in warm—not hot—water; then slightly loosen the jelly at the edge, turning the mold meanwhile from side to side, then place serving dish on top of mold and invert and carefully remove the mold. A delicate jelly cannot be moved easily after it has been unmolded, so that care must be taken to place it evenly on the dish. If before unmolding a lace paper doily is placed evenly over the mold, so that when inverted the doily is between the gelatine mixture and the serving dish, the jelly can be moved at will on the paper.

CAUTION—The liquid quantities in the recipes in this book are based on Wine Measurement (U. S. Standard) and are correct. However, when using the Imperial or Metric System, a quart of which measures more than one quart Wine Measure, this should be taken into consideration and less water or more gelatine used.

Prune
Oriental Cream
(See Page 12)

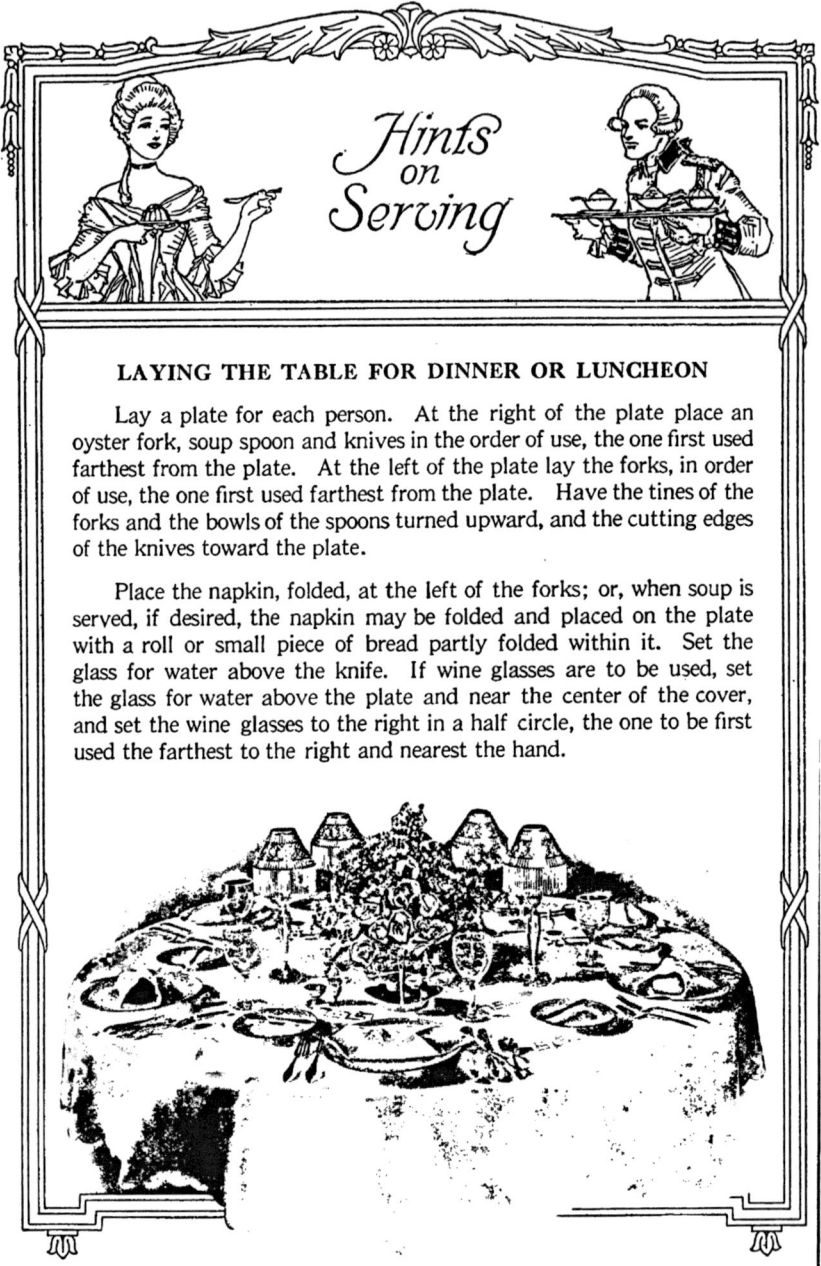

Hints on Serving

LAYING THE TABLE FOR DINNER OR LUNCHEON

Lay a plate for each person. At the right of the plate place an oyster fork, soup spoon and knives in the order of use, the one first used farthest from the plate. At the left of the plate lay the forks, in order of use, the one first used farthest from the plate. Have the tines of the forks and the bowls of the spoons turned upward, and the cutting edges of the knives toward the plate.

Place the napkin, folded, at the left of the forks; or, when soup is served, if desired, the napkin may be folded and placed on the plate with a roll or small piece of bread partly folded within it. Set the glass for water above the knife. If wine glasses are to be used, set the glass for water above the plate and near the center of the cover, and set the wine glasses to the right in a half circle, the one to be first used the farthest to the right and nearest the hand.

SEATING GUESTS AT TABLE

The success of a formal dinner depends greatly upon the selection of the guests and the order in which they are seated at the table.

The host and hostess should sit directly opposite each other. The ladies and gentlemen should sit in alternate seats between the host and hostess. The alternate arrangement may be followed with six or ten persons, but not when eight or twelve are present.

When dinner is announced the host should enter the dining room with the guest of honor. Then the men guests should escort the ladies into the room. The hostess with the man guest of honor should be the last to enter. The guests should stand back of their chairs until the hostess is seated, and each man should adjust the chair for the lady he is escorting and see that she is comfortably seated before he takes his place at her side.

SERVING FORMAL MEALS

Meals are served either from the dining table or by waitress or butler from the serving table and pantry. The custom now is to have the dishes passed to each guest, the meats, etc., being carved into convenient size for the purpose. They are passed to the left of the guests. All dishes, glasses, etc., not again required on the table should be removed from the left when the next course is served.

SERVING THE SALAD

Salad, served with the roast or game (on small chilled plates), is eaten with the fork provided for that course. A salad fork is supplied for a salad served as a separate course. This is placed when the table is laid, according to the position of the salad in the menu, or just before the salad is passed.

SERVING THE DESSERT

For the dessert course, spoons or forks are usually supplied when the table is set, or if one prefers they may be placed for this course after the table has been cleared. They are laid at the right of the space to be occupied by the plate. When serving the dessert with but one maid in attendance, and empty plates or plates with finger bowls are to be set before the guests, and the dessert to be brought in afterwards, place the plates before the silver. If the dessert is to be brought in on individual plates, place the silver, then bring in the dessert.

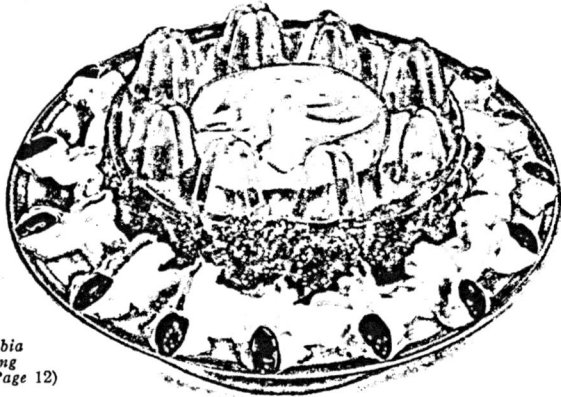

Columbia
Pudding
(See Page 12)

Recipes

IMPORTANT—*Lemon Juice is used in a number of recipes in this book. For those who prefer our* **Acidulated** *package, the* **Lemon Flavor** *contained therein may be used in place of lemon juice. In some cases the housekeeper will have to use her own judgment as to how much to use and flavor the dish according to taste.*

LEMON JELLY

1 envelope **Knox** Sparkling Gelatine. 2 cups boiling water.
1 cup cold water. ¼ cup sugar. ⅓ cup lemon juice.

Soak gelatine in cold water five minutes, and dissolve in boiling water. Add sugar and stir until dissolved; then add lemon juice. Strain through cheese cloth into molds, first dipped in cold water, and chill.

NOTE—*To color the above, or any other jelly, pink, use the vegetable color tablet found in each package, after dissolving it in a little hot water. Fruit juices may also be used to make a colored jelly.*

ORANGE JELLY

1 envelope **Knox** Sparkling Gelatine. 1 cup sugar. 1 cup orange juice.
⅓ cup cold water. 2 cups boiling water. 2 tablespoonfuls lemon juice.

Make same as Lemon Jelly.

COFFEE JELLY

1 envelope **Knox** Sparkling Gelatine. ¾ cup sugar.
⅓ cup cold water. Juice of one lemon.
3 cups clear strong coffee. (½ cup sherry wine if desired).

Soak the gelatine in the cold water five minutes and dissolve in the hot coffee; add lemon juice and sugar, stir until dissolved. When cool strain over wine, if used, and turn into a mold, first dipped in cold water. Serve with whipped cream.

LEMON JELLY WITH BERRIES

Turn two-thirds Lemon Jelly mixture in border mold, first dipped in cold water, and when mixture begins to stiffen garnish with blackberries, and add remaining mixture. Chill thoroughly, remove from mold to serving dish, and fill center with blackberries. Strawberries or raspberries may be used in place of blackberries.

Lemon Jelly
with Berries

GRAPE FRUIT JELLY

1 envelope **Knox** Sparkling Gelatine.
½ cup cold water.
1 cup boiling water.
1 cup sugar.

2 cups grape fruit juice and pulp.
2 tablespoonfuls lemon juice.
½ cup sherry wine.

Soak gelatine in cold water five minutes, dissolve in boiling water and add sugar. Strain, and when mixture begins to thicken add remaining ingredients. Do not pour into molds that have been dipped in cold water until jelly is ready to set in order to avoid settling of pulp. Cut in cubes and arrange in baskets made from grape fruit skins. Garnish each with a teaspoonful of red Bar-le-duc preserve.

CIDER JELLY

1 envelope **Knox** Sparkling Gelatine.
½ cup cold water.
½ cup boiling water.

3 cups sweet cider.
Sugar.

Soak gelatine five minutes in cold water. Dissolve in boiling water and add cider and sugar to taste. Stir until sugar is dissolved, strain into mold, first dipped in cold water, and chill.

DATE CHARLOTTE JELLY

1 envelope **Knox** Acidulated Gelatine.
½ cup sugar.
1 cup cold water.
2 cups boiling water.

1 teaspoonful lemon extract.
1 cup dates.
½ cup pecan nut meats.
½ cup fruit.

Soak gelatine and one-half of the envelope of lemon flavoring in cold water five minutes; add boiling water and sugar, and when sugar is dissolved add extract. When mixture begins to thicken, add dates, nut meats and fruit cut in small pieces. Pour into mold lined with lady fingers and decorate with whipped cream and dates.

WINE JELLY

1 envelope **Knox** Sparkling Gelatine.
½ cup cold water.
1¾ cups boiling water.
1 cup sugar.

1 cup sherry or madeira wine.
½ cup orange juice.
3 tablespoonfuls lemon juice.

Soak gelatine in cold water five minutes and dissolve in boiling water. Add sugar, wine, orange and lemon juice; strain into wet mold and chill.

RHINE WINE JELLY

1 envelope **Knox** Sparkling Gelatine.
½ cup cold water.
2 cups hot water.
3 inch piece stick cinnamon.
5 cloves.
1 allspice berry.

Few gratings from rind of lemon.
¾ cup sugar.
1½ cups Rhine wine.
½ tablespoonful lemon juice.
Few grains salt.

Soak gelatine in cold water five minutes: To hot water add cinnamon, cloves, allspice berry and grated rind; bring to boiling point, and let simmer until reduced to 1½ cups. Strain, add sugar, and let boil two minutes; then add soaked gelatine. As soon as gelatine is dissolved add wine, lemon juice and salt. Strain into molds, first dipped in cold water, and chill.

SAUTERNE JELLY

1 envelope **Knox** Sparkling Gelatine.
½ cup cold water.
1½ cups boiling water.
1 cup sugar.

3 tablespoonfuls lemon juice.
1½ cups Sauterne.
Green coloring.

Soak gelatine in cold water five minutes, and dissolve in boiling water; then add sugar, lemon juice and Sauterne and color green. Turn into a shallow pan, first dipped in cold water, having mixture three-fourths of an inch in depth. Chill, remove from pan to board and cut in cubes.

GRAPE JUICE JELLY

1 envelope **Knox** Acidulated Gelatine.
½ pint grape juice.
½ cup cold water.
2 cups boiling water.
¾ cup sugar.
1 cup Malaga grapes, skinned, seeded and cut in pieces.

Soak gelatine and one-half of the lemon flavoring in grape juice mixed with cold water five minutes. Add boiling water and sugar, and when beginning to set add grapes. Turn into a mold, first dipped in cold water, and chill. Remove from mold and garnish with candied violets. Serve with or without whipped cream.

RHUBARB JELLY

1 envelope **Knox** Sparkling Gelatine.
½ pink color tablet.
½ cup cold water.
1 lb. rhubarb.
1 cup sugar.
1 cup boiling water.
4 tablespoonfuls lemon juice.
Grated rind of one lemon.

Soak gelatine in cold water five minutes. Cut rhubarb in one inch pieces, add sugar and boiling water, bring to the boiling point and let boil fifteen minutes. Add soaked gelatine, coloring, lemon juice and grated rind. Turn into mold, first dipped in cold water, and chill. Serve with whipped cream.

JELLIED PRUNES

1 envelope **Knox** Sparkling Gelatine.
½ lb. prunes.
2½ cups cold water.
1 cup sugar.
¼ cup lemon juice.

Pick over, wash, and soak prunes for several hours in two cups cold water, and cook in same water until soft; remove prunes, stone, and cut in quarters. To prune water add enough boiling water to make two cups. Soak gelatine in half cup cold water, dissolve in hot liquid, add sugar and lemon juice, then strain, add prunes, mold and chill. Stir twice while cooling to prevent prunes from settling. Serve with sugar and cream.

PINEAPPLE JELLY

1 envelope **Knox** Sparkling Gelatine.
2 cups cold water.
1½ cups pineapple juice (scalded).
2 tablespoonfuls lemon juice.
¼ cup sugar.

Soak gelatine in one cup cold water five minutes. Heat pineapple juice, mixed with remaining water, to boiling point and pour over soaked gelatine; then add sugar and lemon juice. Turn into a mold dipped in cold water, and when beginning to set mold in slices of cooked pineapple, fresh raspberries or strawberries.

NOTE—Fresh pineapple fruit or juice must first be scalded, or the jelly will not harden.

FRUITED SPONGE OR CUP CAKES

½ envelope **Knox** Sparkling Gelatine.
¼ cup cold water.
1 cup sugar.
2 cups grated pineapple.
1 cup thick cream.

Cook pineapple and sugar until thick and set aside to cool. Soak gelatine in cold water five minutes and let stand over boiling water until dissolved. When cool add to stiffly whipped cream, and beat into pineapple. Cut off top of individual sponge or cup cakes, hollow out center and fill with above paste. Replace top of cake and cover whole of cake with frosting made according to the recipe on page 41, and decorate with pieces of pineapple and figs. If desired, any fresh or canned fruit may be used in place of the pineapple for making the paste.

MOLDED PEARS

1 envelope **Knox** Acidulated Gelatine.
½ cup cold water.
1 can pears.
¼ cup sugar.

Drain pears from their syrup and cut in thirds. To syrup add enough boiling water to make 2½ cupfuls, and sugar. Bring to the boiling point, and let boil three minutes. Soak gelatine, half of the lemon flavoring found in the Acidulated package, and part of the pink coloring in cold water five minutes, and dissolve in hot syrup. When mixture begins to stiffen mold in layers with pears between.

Cold Desserts

ORANGE JELLY, FRENCH STYLE

Cut a thin slice from the stem end of as many oranges as are desired, remove juice and pulp and use in making orange jelly. With pinking iron or scissors cut the edge of the orange cups in scallops or points, and let stand in ice water until ready for use. At serving time cut jelly in cubes and fill cups. Garnish with whipped cream, sweetened and flavored, and candied cherries. Serve on green leaves.

CONDENSED MILK PUDDING WITH ORANGE JELLY

1 envelope **Knox** Acidulated Gelatine.   1 cup cold water.
6 tablespoonfuls condensed milk.   ½ teaspoonful lemon flavor.
2 cups hot water.

Add the condensed milk to the hot water. Place on fire, and when beginning to boil add gelatine which has been softened in cold water; also a pinch of salt. When cold, add the lemon flavor dissolved in a tablespoonful of cold water.

Make an Orange Jelly, following directions on page 7. Turn jelly mixture into a fancy mold, first dipped in cold water, and when firm add the condensed milk mixture and set away to harden.

EVAPORATED MILK BLANC MANGE

1 envelope **Knox** Acidulated Gelatine.   1 cup hot water.
1 cup cold water.   ½ teaspoonful lemon flavor.
1 cup evaporated milk.   ⅓ cup sugar.

Proceed as in above recipe, and mold with Orange Jelly.

*Condensed Milk
Pudding*

Knox No. 3 Acidulated Gelatine *is the "Busy Housekeeper's" package. It contains* Lemon Flavor, *the basis of all jellies, and saves time, labor and expense.*

BAVARIAN CREAM No. 1
(Without eggs.)

½ envelope **Knox** Sparkling Gelatine.
¼ cup cold water.
1 pint heavy cream.
⅛ cup sugar.
1 cup scalded milk.
1 teaspoonful vanilla.
1 teaspoonful rum, or
2 tablespoonfuls sherry wine, if desired.

Soak gelatine in cold water five minutes and dissolve in hot milk, then add sugar. Set bowl containing mixture in pan of cold water, and stir until mixture begins to thicken. Add cream, beaten until stiff, and flavoring. Turn into a mold, first dipped in cold water, and chill.

BAVARIAN CREAM No. 2

1 envelope **Knox** Sparkling Gelatine.
½ cup cold water.
2 cups milk.
Yolks of four eggs.
1 cup sugar.
1 pint heavy cream, beaten until stiff.
1 teaspoonful vanilla.

Soak gelatine in cold water five minutes. Make a custard of milk, yolks of eggs and sugar; add soaked gelatine, and when mixture begins to thicken add cream and vanilla. Turn into mold, first dipped in cold water, and chill.

CHOCOLATE BAVARIAN CREAM

Make same as Bavarian Cream No. 1, adding two squares of melted, unsweetened chocolate to the hot milk.

COFFEE BAVARIAN CREAM

Make same as Bavarian Cream No. 1, substituting one-half cup strong boiled coffee in place of one-half cup of the milk, and add one tablespoonful lemon juice.

STRAWBERRY BAVARIAN CREAM

½ envelope **Knox** Sparkling Gelatine.
¼ cup cold water.
1 cup strawberry juice and pulp.
1 tablespoonful lemon juice.
½ cup sugar.
1½ cups heavy cream, beaten until stiff.

Soak gelatine in cold water five minutes, and dissolve by standing cup containing mixture in hot water. Strain into strawberry juice mixed with lemon juice. Add sugar, and when sugar is dissolved set bowl containing mixture in pan of ice water and stir until mixture begins to thicken; then fold in cream. Turn into wet mold lined with strawberries cut in halves, and chill. Garnish with fruit, selected strawberries and leaves. A delicious cream may also be made with canned strawberries.

Strawberry
Bavarian Cream

COCOANUT CREAM

½ envelope **Knox** Sparkling Gelatine.   1 cup shredded cocoanut.
¼ cup cold water.   3 eggs.   Few grains salt.
½ cup sugar.   2 cups milk.   1 teaspoonful vanilla.

Soak gelatine in cold water five minutes. Make custard of yolks of eggs, sugar and milk; remove from range and add soaked gelatine. When mixture begins to set, add cocoanut, whites of eggs beaten until stiff, salt and flavoring. Line a mold with sections of orange, pour in mixture and chill.

MACAROON CREAM

½ envelope **Knox** Sparkling Gelatine.   ½ cup sugar.
¼ cup cold water.   Few grains salt.
3 eggs.   ¾ cup pounded macaroons.
2 cups milk.   1 teaspoonful vanilla.

Soak gelatine in cold water five minutes. Make a custard of egg yolks, sugar, salt, and milk. Add soaked gelatine to hot custard, and when nearly cool, add whites of eggs, beaten until stiff, macaroons and vanilla. Turn into individual molds, first dipped in cold water, and chill. For "French Cream" add one square chocolate.

PRUNE ORIENTAL CREAM *(Illustrated on Page 3)*

½ envelope **Knox** Sparkling Gelatine.   ½ pint heavy cream.
¼ cup cold water.   ½ cup milk.
½ cup scalded milk.   ½ cup cooked prunes, cut in pieces.
⅔ cup sugar.   ½ cup chopped figs.
Whites of two eggs.

Soak gelatine in cold water five minutes, dissolve in scalded milk, and add sugar. Strain into a bowl, set in pan containing ice water, and stir constantly until mixture begins to thicken; then add whites of eggs, beaten until stiff, heavy cream, diluted with milk and beaten until stiff, prunes and figs. Turn into a wet mold, the bottom and sides of which are garnished with halves of cooked prunes, and chill. Remove from mold to serving dish, and garnish with whipped cream (sweetened and flavored with vanilla, forced through a pastry bag and tube, and chopped pistachio nuts.

SPANISH CREAM

½ envelope **Knox** Sparkling Gelatine.   ½ cup sugar (scant).
3 cups milk.   ¼ teaspoonful salt.
Whites of three eggs.   1 teaspoonful vanilla, **or**
Yolks of three eggs.   3 tablespoonfuls wine, if desired.

Soak gelatine in one-half cup milk. Scald remaining milk, and pour slowly on the yolks of eggs well beaten. Add sugar and salt and return to double boiler. Cook until mixture thickens somewhat. Remove from stove, and add gelatine and whites of eggs beaten until stiff. Flavor, and turn into individual molds, first dipped in cold water, and chill. Serve with whipped cream. More gelatine will be required if large molds are used.

COLUMBIA PUDDING *(Illustrated on Page 6)*

Cover the bottom of a fancy mold with Wine Jelly mixture. Line upper part of mold with halves of figs, cut crosswise and soaked in jelly mixture five minutes, having seed sides next to mold. When both are set fill with Spanish Cream mixture and chill. When ready to serve remove to serving dish and garnish with whipped cream, sweetened and flavored with vanilla (forced through a pastry bag and tube) and sections of glacéd cherries.

CANTON CREAM

½ envelope **Knox** Sparkling Gelatine.   ½ tablespoonful brandy.
¼ cup cold water.   1 cup milk.   2 tablespoonfuls ginger syrup.
Yolks of two eggs.   Few grains salt.   ¼ cup Canton ginger, cut in pieces.
1 tablespoonful wine.   1 pint heavy cream.

Soak gelatine in cold water, and add to custard made of milk, eggs, sugar, and salt. Strain, chill in pan of ice water, add flavorings, and when mixture begins to thicken add cream, beaten until stiff.

LEMON SPONGE OR SNOW PUDDING

½ envelope **Knox** Sparkling Gelatine.
¼ cup cold water.
1 cup boiling water.
½ cup sugar.
¼ cup lemon juice.
Whites of two eggs.

Soak gelatine in cold water five minutes, dissolve in boiling water, add sugar, lemon juice and grated rind of one lemon, strain, and set aside; occasionally stir mixture, and when quite thick, beat with wire spoon or whisk until frothy; add whites of eggs beaten stiff, and continue beating until stiff enough to hold its shape. Pile by spoonfuls on glass dish. Chill and serve with boiled custard. A very attractive dish may be prepared by coloring half the mixture red with tablet found in each package.

BANANA SPONGE

½ envelope **Knox** Sparkling Gelatine.
¼ cup cold water.
1 cup banana pulp.
2 tablespoonfuls lemon juice.
½ cup sugar.
Whites of two eggs, beaten stiff.
1 dozen blanched Pistachio nuts, finely chopped.

Soak gelatine in cold water five minutes. Put banana pulp, lemon juice and sugar in saucepan, and bring to the boiling point, stirring constantly. Add soaked gelatine, and stir until cool. When mixture begins to thicken, fold in whites of eggs, beaten until stiff, turn into wet mold or paper cases, and sprinkle with chopped nuts.

PINEAPPLE SPONGE (*Illustrated on Page 23*)

½ envelope **Knox** Sparkling Gelatine.
Yolks of three eggs.
Grated rind of one lemon.
2 tablespoonfuls lemon juice.
½ cup sugar.
Few grains salt.
¾ cup grated canned pineapple.
¼ cup cold water.
¼ cup heavy cream.
Whites of three eggs.

Beat yolks of eggs slightly, and add grated rind, lemon juice, sugar, and salt. Cook in double boiler, stirring constantly, until mixture thickens. Remove from range, and add gelatine (which has soaked in cold water five minutes) and pineapple. When mixture begins to thicken, add cream, beaten until stiff, and whites of eggs, beaten until stiff. Turn into a mold, first dipped in cold water, and chill. Remove from mold to serving dish, and garnish with whole and half slices of canned pineapple (around the edge of which there is a piping of whipped cream, sweetened and flavored with vanilla), glacéd cherries, and green leaves.

MOCHA SPONGE

1 envelope **Knox** Sparkling Gelatine.
¼ cup cold water.
2 cups strong boiled coffee.
¾ cup sugar. Whites of three eggs.

Soak gelatine in cold water five minutes and add to hot coffee; then add sugar. Strain into pan, set in larger pan of ice water, cool slightly, then beat, using a wire whisk, until quite stiff. Add whites of eggs, beaten until stiff, and continue the beating until mixture will hold its shape. Turn into a mold, first dipped in cold water. Chill thoroughly, remove from mold and serve with sugar and thin cream.

MAPLE SPONGE

1 envelope **Knox** Sparkling Gelatine.
1½ cups cold water.
2 cups brown or maple sugar.
½ cup hot water.
Whites of 2 eggs.
1 cup chopped nut meats.

Soak gelatine in cold water five minutes. Put sugar and hot water in saucepan, bring to boiling point and let boil ten minutes. Pour syrup gradually on soaked gelatine. Cool, and when nearly set, add whites of eggs beaten until stiff, and nut meats. Turn into mold, first dipped in cold water, and chill. Serve with custard made of yolks of eggs, sugar, a few grains of salt, milk, and flavoring.

CHERRY SPONGE

½ envelope **Knox** Sparkling Gelatine
½ cup cold water.
1 tablespoonful lemon juice.
1½ cups canned cherries.
1 cup canned cherry juice.
½ cup sugar. Whites of two eggs.

Soak gelatine in cold water five minutes and dissolve in hot cherry juice. Add cherries, stoned and cut in halves, sugar and lemon juice. When mixture begins to set add whites of eggs, beaten until stiff. Turn into mold, first dipped in cold water, and chill. Garnish with whipped cream, sweetened, and flavored with vanilla, and chopped cherries. Other canned fruits may be substituted for the cherries

MARSHMALLOW PUDDING

½ envelope **Knox** Sparkling Gelatine. Whites of 3 eggs.
¼ cup cold water.   1½ teaspoonfuls vanilla.
¼ cup boiling water.   Macaroons.
1 cup sugar.

Soak gelatine in cold water five minutes, dissolve in boiling water, add sugar, and as soon as dissolved, set bowl containing mixture in pan of ice water; then add whites of eggs and vanilla and beat until mixture thickens. Turn into a shallow pan, first dipped in cold water, and let stand until thoroughly chilled. Remove from pan and cut in pieces the size and shape of marshmallows; then roll in macaroons which have been dried and rolled. Serve with sugar and cream.

NEWPORT PUDDING

½ envelope **Knox** Sparkling Gelatine. 1½ tablespoonfuls Sauterne.
1 cup boiling water.   1½ tablespoonfuls sherry.
1 cup sugar.   Green coloring.
¼ cup cold water.   Red coloring.
Whites of three eggs.

Put sugar in small saucepan, pour over boiling water, set on range, bring to boiling point, and let boil three minutes. Remove from range and add gelatine which has soaked in cold water five minutes. Beat until mixture begins to stiffen; then add whites of eggs, beaten until stiff, and continue the beating twenty minutes. Divide the mixture into thirds. To first third add Sauterne, to second third add one-half the sherry and color pink; to remaining third add remaining sherry and color green. Arrange in layers in a fancy mold, first dipped in cold water, first the pink, then the white, then the green. Chill thoroughly.

MARSHMALLOW CREAM

½ envelope **Knox** Sparkling Gelatine. 1 cup sugar.
¼ cup cold water.   1 teaspoonful vanilla.
½ cup boiling water.   1 teaspoonful lemon extract.
Whites of four eggs.   1½ squares chocolate.

Soak gelatine in the cold water five minutes. Add boiling water and place over teakettle until dissolved. Cool, but do not chill. Stir sugar into dissolved gelatine. Beat the whites of eggs very light, and to the eggs add the gelatine and sugar, a few spoonfuls at a time, beating constantly. Divide quickly into three parts. To the first part add part of the pink color found in package and flavor with vanilla; to the second part add melted chocolate and vanilla flavoring, and flavor the third part with lemon.

Mold in layers in square mold, adding nuts to the pink part and red cherries to the white. Chill, cut in slices and serve with or without whipped cream or sauce made with the yolks of eggs. Attractive if served with ice cream instead of cake.

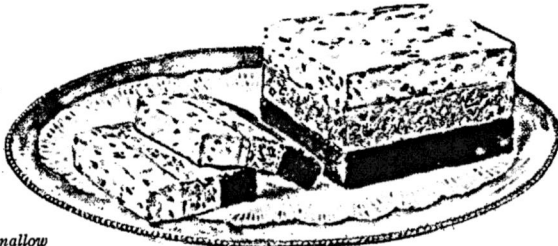

Marshmallow Cream

ANGEL CHARLOTTE RUSSE

½ envelope **Knox** Sparkling Gelatine.	1 cup sugar.
½ dozen rolled stale macaroons.	1 pint heavy cream.
1 dozen marshmallows, cut in small pieces.	Vanilla or sherry.
2 tablespoonfuls chopped candied cherries.	¼ cup cold water.
¼ lb. blanched and chopped almonds.	½ cup boiling water.

Soak the gelatine in cold water, dissolve in boiling water, and add sugar. When mixture is cold, add cream, beaten until stiff, almonds, macaroons, marshmallows and candied cherries. Flavor with vanilla or sherry. Turn into a mold, first dipped in cold water, and chill. Remove from mold and serve with angel cake.

This dessert may be made more elaborate by cutting the top from an angel cake and removing some of the inside, leaving a case with three-fourths inch walls, then filling case with mixture, replacing top of cake, covering with frosting, and garnishing with candied cherries and blanched almonds.

GRAPE JUICE CHARLOTTE RUSSE

½ envelope **Knox** Sparkling Gelatine.	1 tablespoonful lemon juice.
¼ cup cold water.	1½ cups heavy cream, beaten until stiff.
½ cup boiling water.	½ cup sugar.
1 cup grape juice.	Lady fingers.

Soak gelatine in cold water five minutes and dissolve in boiling water. Add grape juice, lemon juice and sugar. Stir until mixture begins to thicken; then fold in cream. Turn into mold lined with lady fingers. Remove from mold and garnish with whipped cream, sweetened, and flavored with vanilla, and candied violets.

CHARLOTTE RUSSE

½ envelope **Knox** Sparkling Gelatine	½ cup cold water.
1½ cups milk.	½ pint heavy cream.
2 eggs.	3 tablespoonfuls powdered sugar.
2 tablespoonfuls sugar.	½ teaspoonful vanilla.
Few grains salt.	Sponge cake.

Scald milk and add gradually to yolks of eggs, slightly beaten, and mixed with sugar and salt. Cook over hot water, stirring constantly, until mixture thickens, then add gelatine, soaked in cold water. Strain and add whites of eggs, beaten until stiff. Set pan in larger pan of ice water and stir, scraping from bottom and sides of pan, until mixture begins to thicken. Then add cream, beaten until stiff, and mixed with sugar and vanilla. Line round paper cases with strips of sponge cake, using muffin rings to keep cases in shape. Fill with mixture and chill. Remove from cases, and garnish tops with four narrow strips of cake, radiating from center, and garnish center with a cube of jelly.

INDIVIDUAL CHARLOTTE RUSSE

Line a sherbet glass with lady fingers, leaving a small space between them. Fill with any Bavarian Cream mixture and chill. Garnish with red and green Maraschino cherries.

Individual
Charlotte Russe

ORANGE CHARLOTTE

½ envelope **Knox** Sparkling Gelatine.　2 tablespoonfuls lemon juice.
¼ cup cold water.　1 cup orange juice and pulp.
½ cup boiling water.　Whites of three eggs.
1 cup sugar.　Lady fingers.

Soak gelatine in cold water five minutes and dissolve in boiling water. Add sugar, and when dissolved add lemon juice. Strain, cool slightly and add orange juice and pulp. When mixture begins to stiffen beat, using a wire whisk, until light; then add whites of eggs, beaten until stiff, and beat thoroughly. Turn into mold lined with lady fingers. One pint whipped cream may be used in place of whites of eggs.

APPLE CHARLOTTE

Make same as Orange Charlotte, using cooked apple pulp in place of orange juice and pulp.

PEACH SNOW BALLS

½ envelope **Knox** Sparkling Gelatine.　½ cup boiling water.
½ cup cold water.　2 tablespoonfuls lemon juice.
1 cup canned peaches, apricots or pine-　Whites of three eggs.
　apple, pressed through a sieve.

Make same as Orange Charlotte, and mold in egg cups.

ALMOND CARAMEL CHARLOTTE RUSSE

½ envelope **Knox** Sparkling Gelatine.　½ lb. blanched almonds, finely chopped.
¼ cup cold water.　1 pint heavy cream, beaten stiff.
1 cup granulated sugar.　1 teaspoonful vanilla.
½ cup boiling water.　1 dozen lady fingers.

Soak gelatine in cold water five minutes. Let stand over hot water until dissolved. Caramelize the sugar and add boiling water very gradually. Cool slightly and add dissolved gelatine. When mixture begins to thicken add nut meats, cream and vanilla. Pour into mold lined with lady fingers and chill.

BLANC MANGE

1 envelope **Knox** Sparkling Gelatine.　1 teaspoonful vanilla, or
3½ cups milk.　1 tablespoonful rum.
¾ cup sugar.

Soak gelatine in half cup milk five minutes. Scald remaining milk with sugar, and add soaked gelatine. Strain, cool slightly, add flavoring and turn into a mold first dipped in cold water, and chill. Serve with currant, strawberry, or any preferred jelly. Accompany with sugar and thin cream, or boiled custard. Substitute cream for the milk and the dish becomes "Ivory Jelly."

CHOCOLATE BLANC MANGE

1 envelope **Knox** Sparkling Gelatine.　1 cup sugar.
½ cup cold water.　Few grains salt.
1 quart milk.　1 teaspoonful vanilla.
2 ozs. grated unsweetened chocolate.

Soak gelatine in cold water five minutes. Scald milk and add sugar, grated chocolate and salt. When sugar is dissolved, add soaked gelatine; then add flavoring. Turn into mold, first dipped in cold water, and chill. Serve with whipped cream, sweetened and flavored with vanilla.

CHARTREUSE OF JELLY

Cut out the center of a round sponge cake, leaving the bottom and sides thick enough to hold a quart of jelly. Prepare a lemon, orange, strawberry or wine jelly, and when it is cold and just ready to form, turn into the cake and set aside in a cool place or on ice. When ready to serve cover the top with the chilled froth from a cup of double cream and a cup of milk beaten with a whip churn. Flavor the cream with vanilla or wine and add one-fourth cup of confectioner's sugar before whipping.

GRAPE JUICE SOUFFLÉ

1 envelope **Knox** Sparkling Gelatine. Whites of four eggs.
1 pint grape juice, sweetened. ¾ cup heavy cream.

Soak gelatine in grape juice ten minutes, then heat in double boiler until gelatine has dissolved. Strain into bowl set in saucepan containing ice water, and when mixture begins to thicken, fold in whites of eggs beaten until stiff. Half fill individual mold, first dipped in cold water, with mixture. To remainder add cream, beaten until stiff. Fill molds with cream mixture, and chill. Remove from molds to serving dish, and garnish with whipped cream (sweetened and flavored delicately with vanilla), candied violets and green leaves.

COFFEE SOUFFLÉ

½ envelope **Knox** Sparkling Gelatine. ⅛ teaspoonful salt
1½ cups strong boiled coffee. 3 eggs.
⅛ cup milk. ½ teaspoonful vanilla.
⅓ cup sugar.

Soak gelatine in one-half cup cold coffee. Mix remaining coffee, milk and one-half of the sugar and heat in double boiler. Add remaining sugar, salt and yolks of eggs, slightly beaten. Cook until mixture thickens. Remove from range, add softened gelatine, whites of eggs beaten until stiff, and vanilla. Mold, chill, and serve with cream.

RICE MOLD WITH PINEAPPLE

½ envelope **Knox** Sparkling Gelatine. Few grains salt.
¼ cup cold water 1 cup cooked rice.
½ cup scalded pineapple juice. 1 cup whipped cream.
⅓ cup sugar. 1 tablespoonful lemon juice.

Soak gelatine in cold water five minutes, and dissolve by standing cup in hot water. Add pineapple juice, sugar and salt to rice. Strain into this the gelatine, and mix thoroughly; cool slightly, and add whipped cream and lemon juice. Turn into mold lined with slices of canned pineapple. Chill, and serve with or without whipped cream. Other fruits may be used in place of pineapple.

AN EASTER DESSERT

1 envelope **Knox** Sparkling Gelatine. ¼ cup sugar.
¼ cup cold water. 1 teaspoonful vanilla.
2½ cups milk or cream, scalded. Few grains salt.

Soften the gelatine in the cold water five minutes and dissolve in the hot milk; add the sugar and flavoring. Wash a dozen large eggs, make a pin hole in one end of each shell, a larger opening in the other end, then shake out the contents from the shell; rinse the shells clean and drain; pour the chilled but liquid pudding through a funnel into the shells and set them in an upright position in a pan of broken ice or salt. When ready to serve, remove the shells and arrange the contents in a nest of orange, lemon or wine jelly, or spun sugar may be used for the nest. Serve with whipped cream.

NOTE—If desired, divide the above mixture into three equal parts, leaving mixture as it is for white eggs, adding dissolved chocolate to the second part to make brown eggs, and to the third part adding a small portion of the pink vegetable color tablet found in each package, after dissolving in a little hot water, to make pink eggs.

NUT FRAPPÉ

½ envelope **Knox** Sparkling Gelatine. 1 cup cream.
¼ cup cold water. ¾ cup milk.
⅓ cup sugar. White of one egg.
1 cup cooked pineapple and strawberries. 1 cup chopped nuts.

Soak gelatine in the cold water five minutes and dissolve over hot water. Add dissolved gelatine to cream, milk and sugar and stir in beaten white of egg. When cold, add the pineapple and strawberries which have been chopped in small pieces, also the chopped nuts. Serve ice cold in sherbet glasses.

ORANGE TRIFLE

1 envelope **Knox** Sparkling Gelatine.
⅓ cup cold water.
1½ cups boiling water.
1 cup sugar.
1 cup orange juice.
Grated rind of one orange.
1 tablespoonful lemon juice.
½ pint heavy cream.

Soak gelatine five minutes in cold water, dissolve in boiling water, add sugar, orange juice, grated rind and lemon juice and strain. Pour one-half the mixture into a shallow pan, dipped in cold water, and chill. Set bowl containing remaining mixture in pan of ice water and stir constantly, until mixture begins to thicken; then fold in heavy cream, beaten until stiff. Turn into a ring mold, first dipped in cold water, and chill. Remove mixture from ring mold to serving dish and garnish with glacéd cherries, cut to represent flowers, and angelica cut to represent leaves and stems. Fill center with first part removed from pan and cut in cubes.

ST. REGIS PUDDING

½ envelope **Knox** Sparkling Gelatine.
½ cup boiling water.
¼ cup cold water.
¼ cup sugar.
¼ cup sherry wine.
¼ cup apricot syrup.
½ tablespoonful lemon juice.
Few grains of salt.
¼ cup seedless raisins.
¼ cup brandy.
¼ cup canned apricots, cut in pieces.

Bring hot water and sugar to boiling point and let boil one minute. Add sherry wine, apricot syrup, lemon juice, salt and gelatine, soaked in cold water. To raisins add brandy and cook in double boiler until raisins are plump. Add to jelly mixture with apricots cut in small pieces. Turn into a mold, chill thoroughly, remove from mold and serve with or without whipped cream, sweetened, and flavored with vanilla.

CHOCOLATE PLUM PUDDING

1 envelope **Knox** Sparkling Gelatine.
¼ cup cold water.
1 cup sugar.
½ teaspoonful vanilla.
1 cup seeded raisins.
¼ cup dates or figs, if desired.
¼ cup sliced citron or nuts, as preferred.
⅙ cup currants.
1½ squares chocolate.
1 pint milk.
Pinch salt.

Soak gelatine in cold water five minutes. Put milk in double boiler, add melted chocolate, and when scalding point is reached add sugar, salt and soaked gelatine. Remove from fire and when mixture begins to thicken add vanilla, fruit and nut meats. Turn into mold, first dipped in cold water, and chill. Remove to serving dish and garnish with holly. Serve with whipped cream, sweetened, and flavored with vanilla.

Chocolate Plum Pudding

IMPORTANT—Lemon Juice is used in a number of recipes in this book. For those who prefer our **Acidulated** *package, the* **Lemon Flavor** *contained therein may be used in place of lemon juice. In some cases the housekeeper will have to use her own judgment as to how much to use and flavor the dish according to taste.*

MACEDOINE PUDDING

¾ tablespoonful **Knox** Sparkling Gelatine.
1 tablespoonful cold water.
2 tablespoonfuls boiling water.
¼ cup Maraschino cherries.
½ cup English walnut meats, cut in pieces.
½ lb. marshmallows, cut in pieces.
1 cup heavy cream.
2 tablespoonfuls powdered sugar.
½ teaspoonful vanilla.

Soak gelatine in cold water five minutes and dissolve in boiling water. Beat cream until stiff, add powdered sugar, vanilla and dissolved gelatine. When mixture begins to stiffen, add chopped cherries, nut meats and marshmallows. Turn into mold, first dipped in cold water, and chill.

PEACH CABINET PUDDING

½ envelope **Knox** Sparkling Gelatine.
1 can peaches.
½ cup powdered sugar.
2 tablespoonfuls sherry wine.
1 tablespoonful brandy.
2 tablespoonfuls cold water.
2 cups milk.
Yolks of three eggs.
Whites of three eggs.
⅓ cup sugar.
⅛ teaspoonful salt.

Drain peaches, cut in quarters, sprinkle with powdered sugar and pour over sherry and brandy. Make a custard of milk, egg yolks, sugar and salt, and just before removing from fire add gelatine soaked in cold water. Strain, and when slightly cooled add one-half cup liquor drained from peaches. Stir until mixture begins to thicken, then add whites of eggs, beaten stiff. Line a mold with peaches, pour in custard and chill.

ROYAL PUDDING

½ envelope **Knox** Sparkling Gelatine.
¼ cup cold water.
2 cups scalded milk.
Yolks of three eggs.
⅓ cup sugar.
⅛ teaspoonful salt.
1 tablespoonful brandy or ½ teaspoonful vanilla.
5 lady fingers.
6 macaroons.

Soak gelatine in cold water five minutes, and add to custard made of milk, eggs sugar and salt. Strain, cool slightly and add flavoring. Place mold in pan of ice water. Decorate with candied cherries and angelica; cover with mixture, adding carefully by spoonfuls. When firm, add layer of lady fingers, first soaked in custard, then layer of macaroons, also soaked in custard. Repeat, care being taken that each layer is firm before another is added. Chill, remove to serving dish and garnish with whipped cream, sweetened, and flavored with vanilla, and candied cherries.

Apple and Grape Fruit Salad (See Page 29)

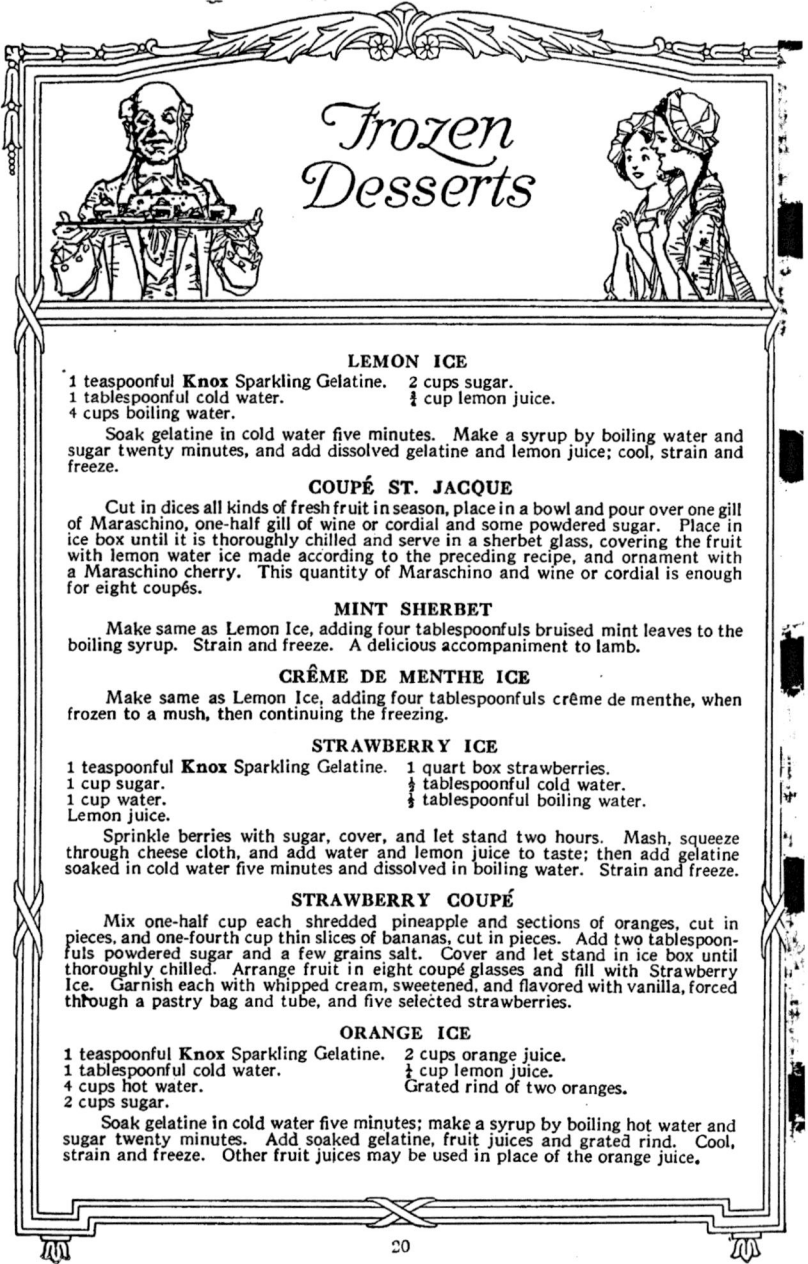

Frozen Desserts

LEMON ICE

1 teaspoonful **Knox** Sparkling Gelatine.	2 cups sugar.
1 tablespoonful cold water.	¼ cup lemon juice.
4 cups boiling water.	

Soak gelatine in cold water five minutes. Make a syrup by boiling water and sugar twenty minutes, and add dissolved gelatine and lemon juice; cool, strain and freeze.

COUPÉ ST. JACQUE

Cut in dices all kinds of fresh fruit in season, place in a bowl and pour over one gill of Maraschino, one-half gill of wine or cordial and some powdered sugar. Place in ice box until it is thoroughly chilled and serve in a sherbet glass, covering the fruit with lemon water ice made according to the preceding recipe, and ornament with a Maraschino cherry. This quantity of Maraschino and wine or cordial is enough for eight coupés.

MINT SHERBET

Make same as Lemon Ice, adding four tablespoonfuls bruised mint leaves to the boiling syrup. Strain and freeze. A delicious accompaniment to lamb.

CRÈME DE MENTHE ICE

Make same as Lemon Ice, adding four tablespoonfuls crème de menthe, when frozen to a mush, then continuing the freezing.

STRAWBERRY ICE

1 teaspoonful **Knox** Sparkling Gelatine.	1 quart box strawberries.
1 cup sugar.	½ tablespoonful cold water.
1 cup water.	½ tablespoonful boiling water.
Lemon juice.	

Sprinkle berries with sugar, cover, and let stand two hours. Mash, squeeze through cheese cloth, and add water and lemon juice to taste; then add gelatine soaked in cold water five minutes and dissolved in boiling water. Strain and freeze.

STRAWBERRY COUPÉ

Mix one-half cup each shredded pineapple and sections of oranges, cut in pieces, and one-fourth cup thin slices of bananas, cut in pieces. Add two tablespoonfuls powdered sugar and a few grains salt. Cover and let stand in ice box until thoroughly chilled. Arrange fruit in eight coupé glasses and fill with Strawberry Ice. Garnish each with whipped cream, sweetened, and flavored with vanilla, forced through a pastry bag and tube, and five selected strawberries.

ORANGE ICE

1 teaspoonful **Knox** Sparkling Gelatine.	2 cups orange juice.
1 tablespoonful cold water.	¼ cup lemon juice.
4 cups hot water.	Grated rind of two oranges.
2 cups sugar.	

Soak gelatine in cold water five minutes; make a syrup by boiling hot water and sugar twenty minutes. Add soaked gelatine, fruit juices and grated rind. Cool, strain and freeze. Other fruit juices may be used in place of the orange juice.

VANILLA PHILADELPHIA ICE CREAM

½ envelope **Knox** Sparkling Gelatine.   2 cups sugar.
½ cup cold milk.   2 tablespoonfuls vanilla.
1 quart scalded milk.   Few grains salt.
1 quart cream.

Soak gelatine in cold milk five minutes and dissolve in scalded milk. Add sugar, and when sugar is dissolved strain mixture into cream, and add flavoring. Freeze, using three parts finely crushed ice to one part rock salt. Serve with maple sauce and chopped pecan nut meats. If part of the cream is whipped and added when partly frozen, it will improve it.

CHOCOLATE ICE CREAM

1 teaspoonful **Knox** Sparkling Gelatine.   1 quart thin cream.
2 tablespoonfuls cold water.   1 cup sugar.
1½ squares unsweetened chocolate.   Few grains salt.
½ cup boiling water.   1 tablespoonful vanilla.

Soak gelatine in cold water five minutes. Melt chocolate and add boiling water gradually, while stirring constantly. Add soaked gelatine, and when dissolved add remaining ingredients. Freeze.

CARAMEL ICE CREAM

1 teaspoonful **Knox** Sparkling Gelatine.   1½ cups sugar.
1 quart milk.   ⅛ teaspoonful salt.
1 pint cream.   1 tablespoonful vanilla.

Soak the gelatine in a little cold milk ten minutes. Caramelize one cup sugar by putting in a granite saucepan and place over hot fire, stirring constantly until melted and of the color of maple syrup. Add one cup hot water and simmer on back of stove until of the consistency of a thick syrup. Add ½ cup sugar to the balance of the milk and scald. Add dissolved gelatine, salt and the caramel. When cold add flavoring and cream; strain and freeze. If preferred, the cream may be whipped and added when the mixture is partly frozen.

NEAPOLITAN ICE CREAM

½ envelope **Knox** Sparkling Gelatine.   2 cups sugar.
½ cup cold milk.   1 quart thin cream.
3½ cups scalded milk.   Whites of three eggs.
Yolks of three eggs.   3 tablespoonfuls vanilla.

Soak gelatine in cold water five minutes. Make custard of milk, yolks of eggs and sugar. Add soaked gelatine and cream, and strain. When cold, add vanilla and freeze to a mush. Add whites of eggs, beaten until stiff, and continue the freezing. Serve with Chocolate Sauce and chopped walnut meats.

CANTALOUPE FRAPPÉ

1 teaspoonful **Knox** Sparkling Gelatine.   ½ teaspoonful salt.
¼ cup cold water.   ½ cup sherry wine.
2 large cantaloupes.   1 teaspoonful lemon juice.
½ cup sugar.

Soak gelatine in cold water five minutes. Dissolve over hot water and strain into cantaloupe pulp, of which there should be two cups. Add remaining ingredients and freeze. Serve in the rind of the melons, cut to represent baskets with or without handles. To prepare the cantaloupe pulp, remove seeds, scrape pulp from rind and force through a purée strainer.

CRANBERRY FRAPPÉ

½ envelope **Knox** Sparkling Gelatine.   1 quart cranberries.
1 cup cold water.   2½ cups sugar.
3 cups boiling water.   4 tablespoonfuls lemon juice.

Soak gelatine in cold water five minutes. Cook cranberries in boiling water until soft; then force through a purée strainer. Add soaked gelatine, sugar and lemon juice, and freeze. A delicious accompaniment to roast turkey.

CUSTARD ICE CREAM

1 teaspoonful **Knox** Sparkling Gelatine.   1 cup sugar (scant measure).
1 quart milk.   1 teaspoonful vanilla.
3 eggs.   Few grains salt.

Soak gelatine in two tablespoonfuls of milk. Make a custard of the milk, yolks of eggs, sugar and salt, and dissolve the gelatine in the hot custard. Strain, and when cold add flavoring and freeze to a mush. Add whites of eggs, beaten until stiff, and continue the freezing.

FRUIT SHERBET
(*Economical*)

½ envelope **Knox** Sparkling Gelatine (scant measure).
1½ cups sugar.   3 cups rich milk.
1 orange.   1 lemon.

Grate the outside of both orange and lemon. Squeeze out the juice and add to this the sugar. Soak the gelatine in part of a cup of milk for five minutes, and dissolve by standing in pan of hot water. Stir into the rest of the milk. When it begins to freeze add the fruit juice and sugar, and fruit of any kind if desired. This makes a large allowance for five persons.

MILK SHERBET

1 teaspoonful **Knox** Sparkling Gelatine.   1½ cups sugar.
1 quart milk.   Juice of three lemons.

Soak gelatine in one-half cup of the milk five minutes. Dissolve over hot water and strain into remainder of milk. Mix lemon juice and sugar, add slowly to milk mixture, and freeze. For a richer sherbet use half cream and half milk.

GRAPE JUICE SHERBET

½ envelope **Knox** Sparkling Gelatine.   1 pint grape juice.
½ cup cold water.   4 tablespoonfuls lemon juice.
1½ cups boiling water.   ½ cup orange juice.
1 cup sugar.

Soak gelatine in cold water five minutes. Make a syrup by boiling sugar and hot water ten minutes, and add soaked gelatine. Cool slightly and add fruit juices; then freeze. Serve in sherbet glasses and garnish with candied violets or fruit, if desired.

Grape Juice Sherbet

Knox No. 3 Acidulated Gelatine *is the "Busy Housekeeper's" package. It contains* **Lemon Flavor,** *the basis of all jellies, and saves time, labor and expense.*

ORANGE CREAM SHERBET

1 teaspoonful **Knox** Sparkling Gelatine.	1½ cups orange juice.
½ cup cold water.	1 pint heavy cream.
1½ cups boiling water.	½ cup sugar.
1½ cups sugar.	2 eggs.
Grated rind of two oranges.	Few grains salt.
1 cup lemon juice.	

Soak gelatine in cold water five minutes. Dissolve gelatine and sugar in boiling water; add orange rind, lemon juice and orange juice. Turn into ice cream freezer and freeze to a mush. Beat cream until stiff, and add sugar and salt. Separate yolks from whites of eggs. Beat yolks until thick and lemon-colored and whites until stiff, and add to cream. Turn into frozen mixture and continue the freezing.

WATERMELON SHERBET

½ envelope **Knox** Sparkling Gelatine.	2 cups sugar.
½ cup cold water.	1 cup orange juice.
4 cups hot water.	2 cups watermelon cubes.

Soak gelatine in cold water for five minutes. Make syrup by boiling hot water and sugar ten minutes and add soaked gelatine and orange juice. Strain, chill and freeze to mush. Add watermelon cubes and let stand one hour.

GRAPE FRUIT SHERBET

½ teaspoonful **Knox** Sparkling Gelatine.	2 cups grape fruit juice.
1 tablespoonful cold water.	2 tablespoonfuls lemon juice.
1 cup boiling water.	Few grains salt.
¾ cup sugar.	

Soak gelatine in cold water five minutes. Make a syrup by boiling water and sugar one minute. Add soaked gelatine, cool slightly and add remaining ingredients. Strain and freeze, using three parts finely crushed ice and one part rock salt.

CLUFF PUNCH

1 teaspoonful **Knox** Sparkling Gelatine.	4 tablespoonfuls lemon juice.
4 cups cold water.	½ tablespoonful rum.
2 cups sugar.	1 cup champagne.
Juice of six oranges.	¼ cup brandy.

Soak gelatine in two tablespoonfuls of cold water five minutes. Make a syrup by boiling the remaining water and sugar twenty minutes. Add soaked gelatine, cool and add fruit juices. Freeze to a mush, then add rum, champagne and brandy, and continue freezing. Let stand two hours.

Pineapple Sponge (See Page 13)

PINEAPPLE MOUSSE

1 teaspoonful **Knox** Sparkling Gelatine. ¾ cup sugar.
3 tablespoonfuls cold water. 1 tablespoonful lemon juice.
1 cup scalded pineapple juice. 1 pint heavy cream.

Soak gelatine in cold water five minutes and dissolve in hot pineapple juice. Add sugar and lemon juice, and when cool add cream beaten stiff. Beat mixture until stiff, using an egg beater, and fill wet mold to overflowing with mixture. Adjust cover, pack in rock salt and finely crushed ice, using equal parts, and let stand four hours. Remove from mold to serving dish and garnish with half slices of canned pineapple and candied cherries.

CHOCOLATE MOUSSE

½ envelope **Knox** Sparkling Gelatine. 1 cup sugar.
¼ cup cold water. 2½ cups heavy cream.
½ cup boiling water. 1 teaspoonful vanilla.
2 squares unsweetened chocolate.

Soak gelatine in cold water five minutes. Melt chocolate in boiling water and add soaked gelatine; then add sugar and vanilla. Cool and add cream, beaten stiff. Fill a chilled mold with mixture, having mixture overflow mold, adjust cover, pack in rock salt and finely crushed ice, using equal parts, and let stand four hours.

RASPBERRY MOUSSE

1 teaspoonful **Knox** Sparkling Gelatine. 3 tablespoonfuls sugar.
¼ cup cold water. ¼ cup boiling water. 1 cup raspberry juice.
1 pint heavy cream. Few grains salt.

Soak gelatine in cold water five minutes, dissolve in boiling water and cool. Beat cream until stiff and add dissolved gelatine and remaining ingredients and whole berries if desired. Fill chilled mold with mixture, adjust cover, pack in rock salt and finely crushed ice, using equal parts, and let stand three hours.

CAFÉ À LA CARLOS

½ envelope **Knox** Sparkling Gelatine. 1 cup sugar.
¼ cup cold water. Yolks of three eggs.
1 cup strong coffee, boiled. 1 pint heavy cream, beaten stiff.

Soak gelatine in cold water five minutes. Make a custard of coffee, sugar and yolks of eggs, and add soaked gelatine. Cool, add cream and freeze. Serve in parfait glasses; garnish with whipped cream, sweetened, and flavored with vanilla, forced through a pastry bag and tube, and glacéd cherries or any fancy fruit.

MARRON BISQUE

½ envelope **Knox** Sparkling Gelatine. 1 pint heavy cream.
½ cup cold milk. 1 cup sugar.
½ cup scalded milk. 1 teaspoonful vanilla.
2 eggs. 1 cup prepared French chestnuts.

Soak gelatine in cold milk ten minutes. Add yolks of eggs, slightly beaten, to scalded milk; then add soaked gelatine. Add sugar and vanilla to cream and combine mixtures; then add whites of eggs, beaten until stiff, and chestnuts. Fill mold with mixture, having mixture overflow mold, adjust cover, pack in salt and ice, using equal parts, and let stand three and one-half hours.

BAKED ICE CREAM

Whites of six eggs. Thin sheet sponge cake.
6 tablespoonfuls powdered sugar. ¼ teaspoonful vanilla.
2 quarts vanilla Philadelphia brick ice
  cream.

Beat whites of eggs until stiff and add sugar gradually while beating constantly, then add vanilla. Cover a board with letter paper, lay on sponge cake, turn ice cream on cake, having cake extend one-fourth inch beyond cream. Cover with meringue and spread smoothly. Place on grate and brown meringue quickly in hot oven; slip from paper to serving dish.

PINEAPPLE BOMB

PART I.

½ teaspoonful **Knox** Sparkling Gelatine.
1 can sliced pineapple.
1 cup water.
⅓ cup sugar.
1 tablespoonful cold water.
Pink coloring.

Press juice from pineapple and add to syrup made by cooking water and sugar five minutes; then add gelatine soaked in cold water five minutes. Color pink, strain and freeze.

PART II.

½ tablespoonful **Knox** Sparkling Gelatine.
½ cup medium cream.
Yolks of two eggs.
3 tablespoonfuls sugar.
1 tablespoonful cold water.
Few grains salt.
⅓ teaspoonful vanilla.
¼ cup powdered sugar.
1 cup candied fruit, cherries and plums.
Brandy.
1 cup heavy cream.

Scald medium cream and add yolks of eggs, slightly beaten, mixed with sugar and salt. Cook in double boiler until mixture thickens, add gelatine soaked in cold water and strain. Set bowl containing mixture in pan containing cold water, and when beginning to thicken fold in heavy cream, beaten until stiff, vanilla, powdered sugar, candied fruit, cut in pieces and soaked several hours in brandy to cover. Line a three-pint brick mold, first dipped in cold water, with Part I and fill with Part II, to overflow mold. Adjust cover pack in rock salt and finely crushed ice, using equal parts, and let stand two hours.

ANGEL PARFAIT WITH CANDIED FRUIT

1 teaspoonful **Knox** Sparkling Gelatine.
Whites of two eggs, beaten dry.
1½ cups heavy cream, beaten light.
3 tablespoonfuls wine or thick syrup.
2 tablespoonfuls cold water.
½ cup candied fruit cut fine.
½ cup granulated sugar.
½ cup water.

Soak the gelatine in the cold water five minutes or longer. Boil the sugar and half cup of water to the soft ball degree (as in making boiled frosting), pour in a fine stream onto the whites of eggs, beating constantly meanwhile; add the gelatine, stir over cold or ice water until the mixture is cold and begins to set, then fold in the cream and the fruit and flavoring. The fruit will be softer if soaked in the wine or syrup some hours or over night. Turn into a quart mold, lined with paper, cover securely and let stand in equal measures of ice and salt about three hours.

NESSELRODE PUDDING

½ envelope **Knox** Sparkling Gelatine.
¼ cup cold water.
2 cups milk.
Yolks of four eggs.
1½ cups sugar.
¼ teaspoonful salt.
1 pint cream.
1 cup prepared French chestnuts, broken in pieces.
1 cup pineapple syrup.
1 cup candied fruits, cut in pieces and soaked in wine to cover.
1 teaspoonful vanilla.
1 tablespoonful sherry wine, if desired.

Soak gelatine in cold water five minutes. Make a custard of milk, yolks of eggs, sugar and salt, and add soaked gelatine. Cool and add remaining ingredients. Fill wet mold to overflowing with mixture, adjust cover, pack in rock salt and finely crushed ice, and let stand three hours.

RICE PARFAIT

½ envelope **Knox** Sparkling Gelatine.
2 cups hot boiled rice.
1½ cups milk.
1 cup cream.
1 cup sugar.
¼ teaspoonful salt.
1 cup chopped nut meats.
1 teaspoonful vanilla.

Soak gelatine in milk ten minutes and dissolve in hot rice. Add sugar and salt, and when cool fold in cream, beaten until stiff. Add nut meats and flavoring. Turn into a mold, and pack in ice and salt.

MAPLE RICE PARFAIT

Make same as Rice Parfait, using maple sugar in place of white sugar.

Salads and Savories

PERFECTION SALAD

1 envelope **Knox** Sparkling Gelatine.
½ cup cold water.
½ cup mild vinegar.
2 tablespoonfuls lemon juice.
2 cups boiling water.
½ cup sugar.
1 teaspoonful salt.
1 cup cabbage, finely shredded.
2 cups celery, cut in small pieces.
2 pimentoes, cut in small pieces.

Soak gelatine in cold water five minutes. Add vinegar, lemon juice, boiling water, sugar, and salt. Strain, and when mixture begins to stiffen, add remaining ingredients. Turn into mold, first dipped in cold water, and chill. Remove to bed of lettuce or endive. Garnish with mayonnaise dressing, or cut in cubes, and serve in cases made of red or green peppers, or turn into molds lined with canned pimentoes.
A delicious accompaniment to cold sliced chicken or veal.

TUNA FISH SALAD

½ envelope **Knox** Sparkling Gelatine.
¼ cup cold water.
1 cup tuna fish.
½ cup chopped celery.
½ green pepper, finely chopped.
2 tablespoonfuls chopped olives.
¾ cup boiled salad dressing.
½ teaspoonful salt.
¼ teaspoonful paprika.
2 teaspoonfuls vinegar.
Few grains cayenne.

Soak gelatine in cold water five minutes, and add to hot boiled salad dressing. Cool, and add tuna fish, separated into flakes, celery, pepper (from which seeds have been removed), olives, salt, paprika, vinegar, and cayenne. Turn into six individual molds, first dipped in cold water, and chill. Remove from molds to nests of lettuce leaves, and garnish with slices cut from pimolas, diamond shaped pieces cut from green peppers, celery tips, and watercress.

Tuna Fish Salad

JEWEL SALAD

½ envelope **Knox** Sparkling Gelatine.
½ cup cucumber.
½ cup canned sliced pineapple.
¼ cup cold water.
¼ cup boiling water.   ½ cup sugar.

¼ cup vinegar.
⅛ cup pineapple syrup.
1 tablespoonful tarragon vinegar.
1 tablespoonful lemon juice.
Few grains salt.

Pare, chop, and drain cucumber; there should be one-half cup. Chop and drain pineapple; there should be one-half cup. Mix cucumber and pineapple, and add gelatine, which has been soaked in cold water and dissolved in boiling water; then add remaining ingredients. Turn into individual molds, first dipped in cold water, and chill. Remove from molds to nest of lettuce leaves. Accompany with mayonnaise dressing.

CHEESE SALAD

½ envelope **Knox** Sparkling Gelatine.
½ cup cold water.   2 cream cheeses.
½ cup American cheese, cut in very small pieces.

1 cup heavy cream, beaten until stiff.
¾ teaspoonful salt.
½ teaspoonful paprika.

Soak gelatine in cold water five minutes, and dissolve over hot water. Work cream cheese until smooth, add American cheese, whipped cream, and soaked gelatine. Season with salt and paprika, turn into individual molds, first dipped in cold water, and chill. Serve on lettuce leaves, and garnish with mayonnaise.

CUCUMBER SALAD

½ envelope **Knox** Sparkling Gelatine.
2 cups chicken stock, well seasoned.
1 slice onion.

1 sprig parsley.
2 cucumbers.
Green coloring.

Soak gelatine in one cup stock. To remaining stock add onion, parsley and cucumbers, pared and grated. Cover and let stand two hours. Heat gradually to the boiling point, add gelatine and color light green. Let stand until nearly cold, then strain into individual paper cases or molds, in the bottom of which is a slice of cucumber. Garnish tops with mayonnaise dressing and halves of blanched Jordan almonds.

SALMON MOLD

1 envelope **Knox** Sparkling Gelatine.
2 tablespoonfuls cold water.
Yolks of two eggs.
2 teaspoonfuls salt.
1 teaspoonful mustard.

Few grains cayenne.
1½ tablespoonfuls melted butter
¾ cup milk.
2 tablespoonfuls vinegar.
1 can salmon.

Soak gelatine in cold water five minutes. Mix egg yolks, slightly beaten, with salt, mustard, and cayenne; then add butter, milk, and vinegar. Cook in double boiler, stirring constantly, until mixture thickens. Add soaked gelatine and salmon, separated into flakes. Turn into fish mold, first dipped in cold water, chill, and remove to bed of crisp lettuce leaves.

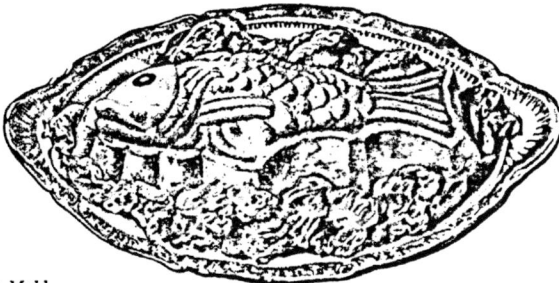

Salmon Mold

LUNCHEON SALAD

1 envelope **Knox** Sparkling Gelatine.	½ cup sugar.
1 cup cold water.	3 tart apples.
1½ cups boiling water.	1 cup celery, cut in small pieces.
⅓ cup lemon juice.	½ cup pecan nut meats.

Soak gelatine in cold water five minutes, and dissolve in boiling water. Add lemon juice and sugar. When mixture begins to stiffen, add apples, sliced in small pieces, chopped celery and broken nut meats. Turn into mold, first dipped in cold water, and chill. Accompany with mayonnaise dressing. This mixture may be served in cases made from bright red apples.

JELLIED CHICKEN

Dress, clean, and cut up a fowl. Put in a stewpan with two slices onion, cover with boiling water, and cook slowly until meat falls from bones. When half cooked, add one-half tablespoonful salt. Remove chicken, reduce stock to two cups, strain, skim off fat, and add one tablespoonful gelatine, soaked in four tablespoonfuls cold water. Decorate bottom of a mold with parsley and slices of hard-boiled eggs. Pack in meat, freed from skin and bone, and sprinkled with salt and pepper. Pour on stock, and place mold under heavy weight. Keep in a cold place until firm. Canned chicken may be used if desired.

HAM MOUSSE

½ envelope **Knox** Sparkling Gelatine.	1 teaspoonful mixed mustard.
¼ cup cold water.	Few grains cayenne.
⅓ cup hot water.	½ cup heavy cream.
2 cups chopped cold boiled ham.	

Soak gelatine in cold water and dissolve in hot water, and add to chopped or ground ham; when cool add mustard, cayenne, and cream, beaten until stiff. Turn into a mold, first dipped in cold water. Chill, remove from mold to serving dish, and garnish with parsley.

CHICKEN MOUSSE

½ envelope **Knox** Sparkling Gelatine.	¾ cup cold cooked chicken.
Yolks of three eggs.	¼ cup Jordan almonds .
¼ teaspoonful salt.	½ teaspoonful salt.
¼ teaspoonful paprika.	Few grains cayenne.
1 cup hot chicken stock.	1 cup heavy cream.
1 tablespoonful cold water.	

Beat yolks of eggs slightly, add salt, paprika, and chicken stock slowly. Cook over hot water, stirring constantly, until mixture thickens; then add gelatine, which has soaked in cold water five minutes. When gelatine has dissolved, strain mixture, and add chicken (using white meat), and blanched almonds, each finely chopped or ground, and forced through a sieve. Season highly with salt and cayenne. Set bowl containing mixture in larger bowl of ice water, and stir until mixture begins to thicken; then fold in cream, beaten until stiff. Turn into mold, first dipped in cold water, and chill. Remove to platter, and garnish top with round and flower shapes of wine, lemon or tomato jelly, and sprig of parsley; garnish sides with round and flower shapes of jelly and diamond shapes of truffle; garnish around base with cubes of jelly.

JELLIED VEGETABLE RING

½ envelope **Knox** Sparkling Gelatine.	1 teaspoonful salt.
¼ cup cold water.	1 cup celery, cut in small strips.
½ cup boiling water.	½ cup shredded cabbage.
¼ cup sugar.	¼ cup canned peas.
¼ cup vinegar.	½ cup small cucumber cubes.
2 tablespoonfuls lemon juice.	

Soak gelatine in cold water five minutes, and dissolve in boiling water; then add sugar, vinegar, lemon juice, and salt. Strain, cool, and when mixture begins to thicken, add vegetables. Turn into a ring mold, first dipped in cold water, and chill. Remove to serving dish, and arrange around jelly thin slices of cold cooked meat. Fill center with boiled salad dressing.

KNOX SALAD (Chicken Cream)

½ envelope **Knox** Sparkling Gelatine. 1 cup cooked chicken, cut in dice.
¼ cup cold chicken stock. 1 cup heavy cream.
¼ cup hot chicken stock, highly seasoned. Salt and pepper.

Soak gelatine in cold stock, dissolve in hot stock, and strain. When mixture begins to thicken, beat, using an egg beater, until frothy; then add cream, beaten until stiff, and chicken dice. Season with salt and pepper. Turn into one-fourth pound baking powder tins, first dipped in cold water, and chill.

Dressing

1½ teaspoonfuls **Knox** Sparkling Gelatine. 2 tablespoonfuls cold water.
Yolks of two eggs. 1 teaspoonful salt.
Whites of two eggs. 1½ teaspoonfuls sugar.
⅛ teaspoonful pepper. Few grains cayenne.
1 teaspoonful mustard. ¼ cup lemon juice.
⅛ cup hot cream. 1½ tablespoonfuls butter.
⅛ cup heavy cream.

Soak gelatine in cold water five minutes, dissolve by standing in hot water, then strain. Beat yolks of eggs, and add salt, sugar, pepper, cayenne, mustard, lemon juice, and cream. Cook over hot water until mixture thickens, stirring constantly, then add butter and gelatine. Add mixture gradually to whites of eggs, beaten until stiff, and when cold, fold in heavy cream, beaten until stiff. Mold and chill. Turn chicken cream from molds, cut in one inch slices, and arrange on lettuce leaves. Put a spoonful of dressing on each slice, and garnish with one-half English walnut meat. Cut celery in small pieces,—there should be three cupfuls. Break into pieces one cup pecan or English walnut meats, and brown in a moderate oven. Mix celery and nut meats, sprinkle with one-half teaspoonful salt, and add to one-half the dressing. Surround each slice of chicken cream with celery and nut mixture. If a simpler dish is required, the celery and nuts may be omitted.

SHRIMP SALAD

½ envelope **Knox** Sparkling Gelatine. 1 can shrimps.
½ cup cold water. 1 tablespoonful capers.
1½ cups chicken stock. 1 cup cooked peas.
2 truffles.

Soak gelatine in cold water five minutes, dissolve in hot chicken stock, and let cool. Cut truffles in slices, and use for garnishing a fish mold (placed in ice water), dipping the truffles into cool stock, and holding in place until set. Cut shrimps in pieces, and mix with truffle trimmings, chopped. To the stock add shrimps, chopped truffles and capers. Fill wet mold with mixture, and chill. Remove from mold to bed of crisp lettuce leaves, and garnish with peas, dressed with French dressing.

APPLE AND GRAPE FRUIT SALAD

(*Illustrated on Page* 19)

Make a grape fruit jelly according to directions on page 8, omitting wine and pulp. When beginning to set add one cup apple finely cut. Turn into a shallow pan, first dipped in cold water, and chill. Remove from pan and cut in cubes. Arrange in cups made from bright red apples and place on crisp lettuce leaves. Garnish with English walnut meats and serve with French dressing.

FRUIT SALAD SUPRÊME

1 envelope **Knox** Sparkling Gelatine. 2 tablespoonfuls lemon juice.
½ cup cold water. ½ cup sugar.
2 cups boiling water. 1 teaspoonful salt.
¼ cup mild vinegar. 3 cups fresh fruit, cut in small pieces.

Soak gelatine in cold water five minutes, and add boiling water, vinegar, lemon juice, sugar, and salt. Strain, and when mixture begins to stiffen, add fruit, using cherries, oranges, bananas, or cooked pineapple, alone or in combination. Turn into mold, first dipped in cold water, and chill. Remove from mold to nest of crisp lettuce leaves, and accompany with mayonnaise or boiled salad dressing.

TOMATO JELLY

1 envelope **Knox** Sparkling Gelatine.	Stalk celery.
½ cup cold water.	2 cloves.
3½ cups tomatoes.	Few grains cayenne.
½ onion.	2 tablespoonfuls tarragon vinegar.
½ bay leaf.	Few grains salt.

Soak gelatine in cold water five minutes. Mix remaining ingredients, except vinegar, bring to boiling point and let boil ten minutes. Add vinegar and soaked gelatine, and when gelatine is dissolved, strain. Turn into a mold, first dipped in cold water, and chill. Remove from mold to bed of crisp lettuce leaves and garnish with mayonnaise dressing, forced through a pastry bag and tube; or the jelly may be cut in any desired shapes and used as a garnish for salads or cold meats.

TOMATO JELLY MOLDED WITH EGGS

Put a border mold in pan of ice water. Dip chilled slices of hard boiled eggs in one-half tablespoonful of **Knox** Sparkling Gelatine, soaked in one-half tablespoonful cold water and dissolved over hot water. Line mold with slices, holding each in place until it becomes set; then fill mold with tomato jelly mixture and chill. Remove from mold, and fill center with crisp lettuce leaves. Accompany with mayonnaise or boiled salad dressing.

TOMATO JELLY SALAD WITH CHEESE
PART I

Use recipe for Tomato Jelly, strain into cups, and chill. Run a knife around inside of molds, so that when taken out shapes may have a rough surface, suggesting fresh tomatoes. Remove from molds, cut in halves crosswise and put between them the cheese mixture as made in Part II. Arrange on serving dish and garnish with rosettes of lettuce and sprigs of parsley. If preferred fresh tomatoes may be used in place of tomato jelly.

PART II

1 teaspoonful **Knox** Sparkling Gelatine.	2 drops tabasco.
1 10c. cream cheese.	Few grains pepper.
1 tablespoonful heavy cream.	Few grains paprika.
¼ teaspoonful salt.	1 teaspoonful cold water.
⅛ teaspoonful Worcestershire Sauce.	1 teaspoonful boiling water.

Mash cheese and add cream, salt, Worcestershire sauce, tabasco, pepper and paprika; then add gelatine, soaked in cold water and dissolved in boiling water. Mold, chill and cut in slices.

*Tomato Jelly
with Cheese*

FROZEN TOMATO CREAM SALAD

½ envelope **Knox** Sparkling Gelatine.
¼ cup cold water.
1 can tomatoes, quart capacity.
2 cloves.
1 allspice berry.
¼ teaspoonful celery seed.

¼ teaspoonful peppercorns.
1 slice onion.
Sprig parsley.
Few grains cayenne.
1 tablespoonful tarragon vinegar.
½ pint heavy cream.

Soak gelatine in cold water five minutes. Cook tomatoes with cloves, allspice berry, salt, celery seed, peppercorns, onion, parsley, and cayenne, ten minutes. Add soaked gelatine, cool slightly, and add vinegar. Freeze to a mush, add heavy cream, beaten until stiff, pack in half-pound baking powder boxes, having mixture overflow boxes, adjust covers, pack in salt and ice, and let stand one and one-half hours. Remove from boxes, cut in slices crosswise, and serve on lettuce leaves. Accompany with salad dressing.

ASPARAGUS SALAD

1 envelope **Knox** Sparkling Gelatine.
1 cup cold water.
2 cups mild vinegar.
Few grains salt.

3 slices onion.
3 cloves.
3 cups asparagus tips.

Soak gelatine in cold water five minutes. Add onion and cloves to vinegar, and bring to boiling point. Strain and add soaked gelatine. When mixture begins to stiffen, add asparagus tips, and turn into mold, first dipped in cold water. Chill and remove to nests of crisp lettuce leaves.

FROZEN FRUIT SALAD

½ envelope **Knox** Sparkling Gelatine.
2 tablespoonfuls cold water.
1 tablespoonful butter.
Yolks of two eggs.
3 tablespoonfuls sugar.
1 teaspoonful salt.
¼ teaspoonful paprika.

Few grains cayenne.
⅔ cup milk.
¼ cup vinegar.
2 tablespoonfuls canned pineapple juice.
1 cup prepared fruit.
1 cup heavy cream.
Lettuce.

Soak gelatine in cold water five minutes. Melt butter, and add yolks of eggs, well beaten, sugar, salt, paprika, and cayenne. Remove from fire and add gradually milk, vinegar, and pineapple juice. Cook in double boiler, stirring constantly until mixture thickens, and add soaked gelatine. Remove from range, and beat two minutes. Cool, stirring occasionally, and when beginning to set add prepared fruit, using Maraschino cherries, cut in small pieces and strained, orange pulp, canned sliced pineapple, cut in small pieces, and cream, beaten until stiff, being careful that the fruit does not settle to the bottom. Pack in a wet brick mold, having mixture overflow mold, adjust cover, and pack in finely crushed ice and rock salt, using two parts ice to one part salt, and let stand two hours. Remove to bed of crisp lettuce leaves, and cut in slices, crosswise, for serving. Accompany with mayonnaise dressing.

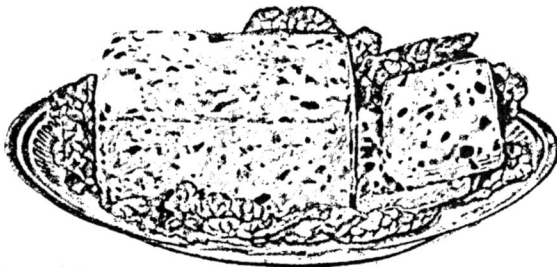

Frozen Fruit Salad

ASPIC JELLY

2 envelopes **Knox** Sparkling Gelatine.	½ cup Madeira wine.
2 tablespoonfuls each carrot, onion, and celery, cut in small pieces.	1 quart brown stock.
	1 cup cold water.
2 sprigs each parsley and thyme.	3 tablespoonfuls lemon juice.
1 stalk savory.	Whites of three eggs, slightly beaten.
2 cloves. 1 bay leaf.	Salt.
⅛ teaspoonful peppercorns.	Cayenne.

Put carrot, onion, celery, parsley, thyme, savory, cloves, bay leaf, peppercorns and wine in saucepan, bring to the boiling point, and let boil eight minutes; then strain. To brown stock add strained liquid, gelatine soaked in cold water five minutes, lemon juice, whites of eggs, slightly beaten, and salt and cayenne to taste. Stir constantly until boiling point is reached, and let stand on back of range twenty minutes; then strain and chill. One-quarter cup brandy may be added if desired.

CHICKEN ASPIC JELLY

Make same as Aspic Jelly, using chicken stock in place of brown stock.

ASPIC JELLY WITH BEEF EXTRACT

1 envelope **Knox** Sparkling Gelatine.	6 peppercorns.
3½ cups cold water. 1 onion.	1 stalk celery.
1 ounce chopped lean raw ham.	1 sprig parsley.
1 teaspoonful beef extract or 2 bouillon cubes.	Bit of bay leaf.
	1 teaspoonful salt.

Soak gelatine in one-half cup cold water five minutes. Bring remaining ingredients, except beef extract and salt, to boiling point, and let simmer ten minutes; then add salt, soaked gelatine and beef extract. Strain through a double thickness of cheese cloth and chill.

MOCK ASPIC

1 envelope **Knox** Sparkling Gelatine.	1 quart cold water.
1 large bunch celery.	¼ cup cold water.
4 slices carrot.	Salt.
2 slices onion.	Cayenne.
2 sprigs parsley.	Lemon juice.
1 sprig thyme.	Whites of two eggs.
⅛ teaspoonful celery seed.	Green coloring.

Wash and cut celery in small pieces. Put in saucepan with carrot, onion, parsley, thyme, celery seed, and one quart cold water, bring to the boiling point, and let simmer one and one-half hours. Strain and cool; there should be two cups liquid. Add gelatine soaked in one-half cup cold water, and season to taste with salt, cayenne and lemon juice; then add whites of eggs, slightly beaten, bring slowly to the boiling point, color light green, and let stand on back of range to clear, then strain and chill.

LOBSTER IN ASPIC

Remove meat from a two-pound boiled lobster, cut in pieces of uniform size, and dress with olive oil, vinegar and cayenne. Mold in aspic jelly mixture, and chill. Remove from mold to nest of crisp lettuce leaves. Garnish with lobster shells and large claws. Accompany with mayonnaise dressing. Sardines may also be molded similarly in Aspic Jelly.

MINT JELLY FOR COLD LAMB

½ envelope **Knox** Sparkling Gelatine.	¼ teaspoonful salt.
⅓ cup cold water.	Few grains paprika.
1 cup sugar.	1 cup finely chopped mint leaves.
1 cup vinegar.	Green coloring.

Soak gelatine in cold water five minutes, and dissolve in syrup made by boiling sugar and vinegar five minutes. Add salt and paprika, color green and strain; then add mint leaves. Let stand five minutes, strain into wet molds and chill.

ORANGE AND ENDIVE SALAD

Force Orange Jelly through a potato ricer. Arrange thin crosswise slices of orange, from which seeds have been removed, on a bed of endive. Surround with jelly, and pour French dressing over all.

JELLIED CELERY

1 envelope **Knox** Sparkling Gelatine.
1 cup cold water.   1½ cups boiling water.
⅓ cup lemon juice.
⅓ cup sugar.

½ tablespoonful grated horseradish root.
¼ teaspoonful salt.
Few grains pepper.   Few grains cayenne.
1 cup finely cut celery.

Soak gelatine in cold water five minutes, and dissolve in boiling water; then add lemon juice, sugar, grated horseradish root, salt, pepper and cayenne. Color light green and strain. When mixture begins to thicken, add celery, turn into mold first dipped in cold water, and chill. Remove to small nests of lettuce leaves, and serve with

French Russian Dressing.—Mix one teaspoonful salt, one-third teaspoonful pepper, few grains cayenne, one-half cup olive oil, two tablespoonfuls vinegar, one-quarter cup tomato catsup, and two teaspoonfuls chives, cut in small pieces.

MUSHROOM BROTH

1 envelope **Knox** Sparkling Gelatine.
1 cup cold water.   5 cups chicken stock.
1 cup mushrooms, broken in pieces.
1 onion, thinly sliced.

1 stalk celery.
½ teaspoonful salt.
Few grains pepper.
3 cloves.

Soak gelatine in cold water five minutes. Place remaining ingredients in stewpan on range, bring to boiling point, and let boil ten minutes. Add soaked gelatine and strain. Serve in bouillon cups, with a spoonful of whipped cream on each.

VEAL LOAF

1 envelope **Knox** Acidulated Gelatine.
1 cup cold water.
2 cups stock, well seasoned.
1 onion, peeled and sliced
1 stalk celery.

2 cups chopped cold cooked veal, ham,
    beef or chicken.
½ cup canned pimentoes, cut in thin strips
½ tablespoonful finely chopped parsley.

Soak gelatine and one-half teaspoonful of the lemon flavoring found in the Acidulated Package in cold water five minutes. Add onion and celery to stock, bring to the boiling point, let boil three minutes, and pour over soaked gelatine. When mixture begins to stiffen, add meat, pimentoes, and chopped parsley. Turn into brick mold, first dipped in cold water, and chill. Remove from mold, and cut in slices for serving.

SWEETBREAD SALAD

½ tablespoonful **Knox** Sparkling Gelatine.
½ cup sweetbread, cut in slices.
½ cup cucumber cubes.
½ cup heavy cream.

1½ tablespoonfuls vinegar.
2 tablespoonfuls boiling water.
Salt.

Mix sweetbread and cucumber cubes and season with salt. Beat cream until stiff and add gelatine which has been soaked in the vinegar and dissolved in the boiling water. Set in pan of ice water, and as soon as mixture begins to thicken add sweetbread and cucumber. Turn into mold, first dipped in cold water, and chill. Serve on lettuce leaves and garnish top with a sprig of parsley.

MEAT OR FISH RELISH

½ envelope **Knox** Sparkling Gelatine.
¼ cup cold water.   ½ teaspoonful salt.
½ teaspoonful celery seed.
½ teaspoonful mustard seed.

½ cup vinegar.
½ cup sugar.
1½ cups finely shredded cabbage.
½ cup thinly sliced onion.

Soak gelatine in cold water, and dissolve in hot vinegar; then add remaining ingredients. Turn into individual molds, lined with canned pimentoes, and chill.

MACEDOINE SALAD

Make Tomato Jelly mixture. Wash, scrape and cut celery stalks in thin slices crosswise; there should be one cup. Wipe, pare, peel and core two large apples, cut in slices and in small pieces. Chop one cup walnut meats, mix celery, apple and nut meats, and moisten with mayonnaise dressing. Put one tablespoonful Tomato Jelly mixture in each individual mold. Then add vegetable and nut mixture and cover with Tomato Jelly mixture. Chill, turn from molds and garnish with watercress.

CRAB SALAD

⅓ tablespoonful **Knox** Sparkling Gelatine.	1 egg.
¼ cup cold water.	½ cup condensed milk (unsweetened).
1½ tablespoonfuls flour.	5 tablespoonfuls lemon juice.
¼ tablespoonful mustard.	2 tablespoonfuls butter.
2 tablespoonfuls sugar.	1 cup crab meat.
½ tablespoonful salt.	½ cup heavy cream.
¼ teaspoonful celery salt.	

Soften gelatine in the cold water. Mix dry ingredients, add egg slightly beaten, condensed milk and lemon juice. Cook over hot water, stirring constantly until mixture thickens. Strain and add gelatine and butter. When it begins to thicken add crab meat and cream beaten until stiff. Turn into buttered molds and chill. Remove to bed of lettuce leaves.

INDIAN SALAD

½ cocoanut, grated.	3 pimentoes.
2 apples, cored and chopped.	1 tablespoonful grated onion.
2 cups celery, chopped.	¼ teaspoonful salt.

Allow small amount of lemon jelly to harden in individual molds, fill with the above salad mixture, and pour liquid lemon jelly over. When hardened, unmold and sprinkle with some of the grated cocoanut, and serve on lettuce leaves with mayonnaise dressing. Garnish with pieces of the bright red pepper.

CORNED TONGUE IN ASPIC

Remove skin from a boiled corned tongue, skewer into shape, and cool; then cover with brown Chaudfroid sauce. When sauce has stiffened, cover with liquid aspic, and when beginning to stiffen, garnish with pistachio nuts, whites of hard boiled eggs, and truffles cut in fancy shapes. Again cover with liquid aspic, and let stand until set. Remove to platter, and garnish with roses made from yolks of hard boiled eggs (moistened with melted butter and seasoned with salt), forced through a pastry bag and tube, and Sauterne jelly, broken up to represent moss. Insert a skewer with a piece of truffle between two pimolas. Garnish at base with Sauterne jelly, broken up to represent moss, and celery, curled to represent feathers. For the brown Chaudfroid sauce, brown one tablespoonful butter, add one and one-half tablespoonfuls flour, and stir until well browned; then pour on gradually, while stirring constantly, one-third cup brown sauce, bring to the boiling point, and add one-fourth cup liquid aspic.

This Corned Tongue illustration is published to show the possibilities of garnishing any meat that is made in jellied form.

Corned Tongue in Aspic

Candies

FRENCH DAINTIES

2 envelopes **Knox** Acidulated Gelatine.   1½ cups boiling water.
4 cups granulated sugar.   1 cup cold water.

Soak the gelatine in the cold water five minutes. Add the boiling water. When dissolved add the sugar and boil slowly for fifteen minutes. Divide into two equal parts. When somewhat cooled add to one part one-half teaspoonful of the Lemon Flavor found in separate envelope, dissolved in one tablespoonful water, and one tablespoonful lemon extract. To the other part add one tablespoonful brandy, if desired, one-half teaspoonful extract of cloves, and color with the pink color. Pour into shallow tins that have been dipped in cold water. Let stand over night; turn out and cut into squares. Roll in fine granulated or powdered sugar and let stand to crystallize. Vary by using different flavors and colors, and adding chopped nuts, dates or figs.

*French
Dainties*

MARSHMALLOWS

1 envelope **Knox** Sparkling Gelatine.   Few grains salt.
1¼ cups water.   1 teaspoonful vanilla.
2 cups fine granulated sugar.

Soak gelatine in one-half the water five minutes. Put remaining water and sugar in saucepan, bring to the boiling point and let boil until syrup will spin a thread when dropped from tip of spoon. Add soaked gelatine and let stand until partially cooled; then add salt and flavoring. Beat until mixture becomes white and thick. Pour into granite pans, thickly dusted with powdered sugar, having mixture one inch in depth. Let stand in a cool place until thoroughly chilled. Turn on a board, cut in cubes and roll in powdered sugar. This recipe makes about one hundred marshmallows. Nuts, chocolate, fruit juices in place of part of the water, or candied fruits chopped may be added—or the plain ones rolled in grated cocoanut before being sugared. Dates stuffed with this confection are delicious.

FIG BARS

2 envelopes **Knox** Gelatine.   ⅓ cup chopped blanched almonds.
2 cups cold water.   1 orange.
2 cups sugar.   1 lemon, or 1 teaspoonful of the lemon
½ pound figs.   flavoring found in Acidulated pack-
3 tablespoonfuls sherry wine.   age dissolved in 3 tablespoonfuls cold
½ cup chopped walnut meats.   water.

Soak gelatine in one cup of the cold water ten minutes. Force figs through a food chopper, add juice of lemon, juice of orange and grated rind of orange, bring to the boiling point and let simmer ten minutes. Put sugar and remaining water in saucepan and when sugar is dissolved add soaked gelatine. Bring to the boiling point and let boil ten minutes; then add fig mixture and boil ten minutes, stirring constantly. Remove from range, add nut meats and sherry wine. Pour into shallow pan, first dipped in cold water, and let stand over night. Cut in pieces two and one-half inches by one-half inch. Roll in powdered sugar.

GINGER CRYSTALS

1 envelope **Knox** Gelatine.   1 cup boiling water.
½ cup cold water.   ½ cup crystallized ginger, cut in small pieces.
2 cups granulated sugar.   1 tablespoonful lemon juice.

Soak gelatine in cold water ten minutes. Put sugar and boiling water in saucepan, place on range, and when sugar is dissolved add soaked gelatine. Bring to boiling point and let boil fifteen minutes. Remove from range and add lemon juice or one-half teaspoonful lemon flavoring found in the Acidulated package, dissolved in one tablespoonful cold water and crystallized ginger. Turn into pan dipped in cold water, having mixture three-fourths inch in depth. Let stand over night, cut in oblong shapes, roll in fine granulated sugar and let stand to crystallize.

COCOANUT FUDGE

½ envelope **Knox** Sparkling Gelatine.   2 cups sugar.   1 cup milk.
3 tablespoonfuls cold water.   ½ tablespoonful butter.
1 cup shredded cocoanut.   1 teaspoonful vanilla.

Soak gelatine in cold water five minutes. Put sugar and milk in saucepan, bring to boiling point and let boil until when tried in cold water a soft ball may be formed. Remove from range, add soaked gelatine, butter and vanilla. Beat until creamy, add cocoanut and turn into a buttered pan.

CHOCOLATE FUDGE

1 envelope **Knox** Sparkling Gelatine.   1 cup chopped nut meats, preferably
1⅓ cups milk.   English walnuts or pecans.
1½ squares unsweetened chocolate.   1 teaspoonful vanilla.
2½ cups sugar.

Soak gelatine in two-thirds cup cold milk ten minutes. Bring sugar and remaining milk to boiling point, add melted chocolate and soaked gelatine, and let boil fifteen minutes. Remove from range, stir until it thickens, add nut meats and vanilla. Turn into pan, first dipped in cold water, let stand until cool, cut in squares and roll in powdered sugar.

PEANUT DAINTIES

1 envelope **Knox** Sparkling Gelatine.	⅓ cup boiling water.
½ cup cold water.	2 cups chopped roasted peanuts.
2 cups light brown sugar.	1 tablespoonful lemon juice.

Soak gelatine in cold water ten minutes. Put sugar and boiling water in saucepan, and when sugar is dissolved add gelatine, bring to the boiling point and let boil fifteen minutes. Remove from range and add one cup peanuts and one tablespoonful lemon juice, or one-half teaspoonful of the lemon flavoring found in the Acidulated package, soaked in one tablespoonful cold water. Turn into pan, first dipped in cold water, having mixture three-fourths inch in depth. Let stand over night, cut in squares and roll in ground peanuts.

MINT PASTE

1½ envelopes **Knox** Sparkling Gelatine.	Green coloring.
2 cups sugar.	4 tablespoonfuls crême de menthe.
2 tablespoonfuls lemon juice.	Few grains salt.

Soak gelatine in two-thirds cup cold water ten minutes. Put sugar and two-thirds cup water in saucepan, bring to the boiling point, add soaked gelatine and let boil twenty minutes. Remove from fire, add remaining ingredients and color green. Turn into a pan (first rinsed in cold water) to one inch in thickness. When set, remove to board, cut in cubes and roll in powdered sugar.

CHRISTMAS CANDY SUPRÊME

¼ envelope **Knox** Sparkling Gelatine.	½ cup Sultana raisins.
2 squares chocolate.	½ cup candied cherries.
3 cups sugar.	½ cup chopped English walnut meats.
1 cup sour cream.	¼ teaspoonful cinnamon.

Soak gelatine in two tablespoonfuls cold water ten minutes. Melt chocolate in saucepan placed in larger saucepan containing boiling water. Add sugar and sour cream alternately, while stirring constantly. Bring to the boiling point and let boil until mixture will form a soft b. ˤ when tried in cold water. Remove from fire, add gelatine, and when it has dissolved add cinnamon, raisins, cherries, cut in small pieces, and nut meats. Beat until creamy and turn into buttered tins, having mixture about 1½ inches deep. Cool, remove from pan and cut in slices for serving. The mixture may be put in individual tins, and when unmolding insert in top of each a sprig of holly. Omit fruit in this recipe and you have Somerville Fudge.

COFFEE CHOCOLATE FUDGE

¼ envelope **Knox** Sparkling Gelatine.	1 cup strong boiled coffee.
2 squares chocolate.	2 tablespoonfuls butter.
2 cups white sugar.	1 teaspoonful vanilla.
1 cup brown sugar.	1 teaspoonful vinegar.
⅛ teaspoonful salt.	

Soak gelatine in two tablespoonfuls cold water ten minutes. Melt chocolate in saucepan placed in larger saucepan containing boiling water. Add sugar and coffee alternately while stirring constantly. Place saucepan containing mixture in direct contact with stove, bring to the boiling point, add butter and let boil until mixture will form a soft ball when tried in cold water. Add gelatine and beat until creamy. Add vanilla and vinegar and turn into a slightly buttered pan. Cool and cut in squares.

TURKISH DELIGHT

1½ envelopes **Knox** Sparkling Gelatine.	Juice of one orange.
½ cup cold water.	Juice of one lemon.
2 cups granulated sugar.	1 tablespoonful rum.
½ cup boiling water.	Red coloring.
Grated rind of one orange.	½ cup chopped nut meats.

Soak gelatine in cold water ten minutes. Put sugar and boiling water in saucepan, bring to the boiling point, add soaked gelatine and let boil twenty minutes. Add flavorings and coloring, strain, add nut meats and turn into a bread pan (first dipped in cold water) to one inch in depth. Let stand until firm, remove to board, cut in cubes and roll in powdered sugar. The rum and nut meats may be omitted.

For the Invalid and

*Individual
Orange Jelly
(See page 40)*

Knox Sparkling Gelatine is a plain, straight product, and the flavoring and coloring are packed in separate envelopes in each package and not mixed with the gelatine. To insure the making of attractive, healthful and appetizing gelatine dishes for the sick and convalescent, one should use Plain Granulated Gelatine, and add pure flavors, sweetening, seasonable fruits, etc. Gelatine dishes are taking an important part in dietetics, and physicians are ordering it very largely in the diet of their patients. The careful practitioner, however, recommends only a wholesome, plain gelatine which is found in Knox Sparkling Gelatine.

PORT WINE JELLY
(Individual)

½ teaspoonful Knox Sparkling Gelatine.
½ tablespoonful cold water. 1 clove.
1 inch piece stick cinnamon.
¼ cup port wine.
1 teaspoonful lemon juice.
½ tablespoonful sugar.

Soak gelatine in cold water three minutes. Cook clove, cinnamon, and port wine ten minutes, in top of double boiler, add soaked gelatine, and as soon as gelatine has dissolved, add lemon juice and sugar. Strain through double cheese cloth, mold and chill.   Remove to serving plate, and garnish with whipped cream, sweetened and flavored with vanilla.

JELLIED CHICKEN BOUILLON
(Individual)

Make a well seasoned stock from a young fowl, adding celery salt or chopped parsley if an additional flavor is desired.

Soak three-fourths teaspoonful Knox Sparkling Gelatine in one tablespoonful cold water five minutes, and dissolve in one tablespoonful boiling water. Add to one-half cup hot chicken stock and chill. Beat slightly with a fork and serve in a bouillon cup.

NOTE — If it is desired to serve this bouillon hot, add gelatine just the same, as it thickens it and gives more body to the broth.

Convalescent's Tray

GRAPE FRUIT JELLY
(Individual)

1 tablespoonful **Knox** Sparkling Gelatine.
1 tablespoonful cold water.
1 tablespoonful boiling water.
1 tablespoonful sugar.
1 cup grape fruit juice.

Soak gelatine in cold water three minutes. Add boiling water and sugar, place over hot water, and let stand until gelatine has dissolved; then add grape fruit juice, strain into a wet mold, and chill.

GRAPE JUICE SPONGE
(Individual)

1 teaspoonful **Knox** Sparkling Gelatine
1 cup grape juice.
1 egg white.
2 tablespoonfuls heavy cream.

Add gelatine to grape juice, place over hot water, and let stand until gelatine has dissolved. Strain, and when mixture begins to stiffen add white of egg, beaten until stiff, and heavy cream, beaten until stiff. Turn into a mold, first dipped in cold water, and chill. Remove from mold, and garnish with whipped cream, sweetened and flavored with vanilla, and candied violets.

CREAM CHICKEN SALAD
(Individual)

4 tablespoonfuls heavy cream.
1 teaspoonful **Knox** Sparkling Gelatine.
1 teaspoonful lemon juice.
Few grains salt.
1 teaspoonful boiling water.
3 tablespoonfuls cold boiled fowl, cut in small cubes.
1 tablespoonful finely chopped parsley.

Beat cream until stiff and add gelatine, soaked in lemon juice three minutes and dissolved in boiling water. When mixture begins to thicken add fowl (using preferably the white meat), mixed with parsley and salt. Turn into an individual mold, first dipped in cold water, and chill. Remove from mold to crisp lettuce leaves and garnish with a sprig of parsley.

Additional Uses for Knox Gelatine

ORANGE JELLY IN SECTIONS OF ORANGE PEEL (*Illustrated on page* 38)
¾ teaspoonful **Knox** Sparkling Gelatine. ½ cup orange juice.
½ tablespoonful cold water. 1 teaspoonful lemon juice.
1 tablespoonful boiling water. 1½ tablespoonfuls sugar.

Cut a circular piece of peel one inch in diameter from the stem end of an orange. Introduce handle of a silver spoon into opening thus made, and remove pulp and juice. Strain juice from pulp, and use in making jelly. The forefinger of the right hand may be of assistance in loosening pulp lying close to skin, which should be discarded, as it is apt to make a cloudy jelly. Proceed same as in making Lemon Jelly. Fill orange with mixture, place in pan, and surround with ice to which a small quantity of water has been added. As soon as jelly is firm, cut in halves lengthwise, and cut halves in thirds, arrange on serving dish on a lace paper doily, and garnish with glacéd cherry.

KNOX MAYONNAISE DRESSING
1 teaspoonful **Knox** Sparkling Gelatine. Yolks of two eggs.
1 teaspoonful mustard, if liked. 4 tablespoonfuls Lemon Juice.
1 teaspoonful salt. Few grains cayenne. 2 cups olive oil.

Mix mustard, salt, sugar and cayenne. Add egg yolks, and when well mixed one-half teaspoonful Lemon Juice; then add gelatine, soaked in one-half tablespoonful Lemon Juice five minutes, and dissolved over boiling water. Cool, and add oil gradually, at first drop by drop, and stir constantly. As mixture thickens, thin with remaining lemon juice. Add oil and lemon juice alternately, until all is used, stirring or beating constantly. If oil is added too rapidly, dressing will have a curdled appearance. Olive oil for the making of mayonnaise should be thoroughly chilled. Mayonnaise should be stiff enough to hold its shape.

NOTE—If preferred, mild vinegar may be used in place of the lemon juice. A little garlic or onion and a teaspoonful of curry powder may be mixed with the dressing to give an added flavor. A small amount of **Knox** *Gelatine added to a cooked dressing improves it and makes it stand up firm and hard.*

BUTTER MIXTURE
NOTE—This mixture is intended for immediate use, and will do the work of two pounds of ordinary butter for table use and for baking cakes, muffins. etc., but is not used for frying purposes.
1 pound good butter. 1 heaping teaspoonful **Knox** Gelatine.
2 pint bottles milk or one quart. 2 teaspoonfuls salt.

Take the top cream of two pint bottles of milk, and add enough of the milk to make one pint.

Soak the gelatine in two tablespoonfuls of the milk ten minutes; place in a dish of hot water until gelatine is thoroughly dissolved.

Cut the butter in small pieces and place same in a dish over hot water until the butter begins to soften; then gradually whip the milk and cream and dissolved gelatine into the butter with a Dover egg beater. After the milk is thoroughly beaten into the butter add the salt to taste.

If the milk forms keep on beating until all is mixed in. Place on ice or in a cool place until hard. If a yellow color is desired, use butter coloring.

CREAM FILLING FOR CAKE
½ envelope **Knox** Sparkling Gelatine. 1 teaspoonful vanilla, or
¼ cup sugar. ½ teaspoonful lemon extract.
⅛ teaspoonful salt. 2 cups scalded milk.
2 eggs. ¼ cup cold milk.

Mix sugar and salt, add egg, slightly beaten, and pour gradually on scalded milk. Cook in double boiler, stirring constantly, until mixture coats the spoon. Add gelatine soaked in cold milk five minutes, and flavoring.

COFFEE CREAM FILLING
Make same as Cream Filling, scalding the milk with two tablespoonfuls ground coffee, and straining before adding sugar, salt and eggs.

RUSSIAN SANDWICHES

Cut bread in one-fourth inch slices, and shape with a fancy cutter. Place one or two small crisp lettuce leaves on one-half the pieces, spread with Russian dressing, cover with remaining pieces of bread, and garnish top of each with one-half pecan nut meat. Arrange on a sandwich plate, covered with a doily, radiating from center. Garnish at center with a few crisp lettuce leaves, to represent a flower, and sprigs of parsley.

RUSSIAN DRESSING

½ teaspoonful **Knox** Sparkling Gelatine.
¾ cup mayonnaise dressing.
3 tablespoonfuls chili sauce.
2 tablespoonfuls pimentoes cut in small pieces.
1 tablespoonful tarragon vinegar.
1 teaspoonful chives, cut in very small pieces.
2 teaspoonfuls cold water.

Mix first five ingredients and fold in gelatine, soaked in cold water five minutes, dissolved by placing over hot water and chill. This dressing may also be used as a salad to serve on lettuce leaves.

FROSTING FOR CAKE

1 teaspoonful **Knox** Sparkling Gelatine.
2 teaspoonfuls cold water.
6 tablespoonfuls hot milk.
2 tablespoonfuls melted butter.
Confectioners' sugar.
1 teaspoonful vanilla.

Soak gelatine in cold water five minutes, and dissolve in hot milk; then add butter. Stir in sugar until mixture is of the right consistency to spread (the amount required being about two and three-fourths cups), and add vanilla.

WHIPPED CREAM

1 teaspoonful **Knox** Sparkling Gelatine.
1 tablespoonful cold water.
1½ cups heavy cream.
¼ cup milk.
⅔ cup powdered sugar.
1 teaspoonful vanilla.
Few grains salt.

Soak gelatine in cold water five minutes, dissolve by placing over boiling water and cool. Mix cream and milk and add dissolved gelatine. Beat until stiff, using an egg beater, and add sugar, vanilla and salt.

GELATINE FLOWERS

¾ tablespoonful **Knox** Sparkling Gelatine.
¼ cup cold water.
⅓ cup cornstarch.
⅔ cup confectioners' sugar.
Vegetable coloring.

Soak gelatine in cold water five minutes. Set bowl containing mixture in saucepan of boiling water and let stand until gelatine has dissolved. Cool slightly and add gradually, while stirring constantly, cornstarch mixed with sugar. Color as desired and shape into fancy forms resembling any flower desired.

PUDDING SAUCE

½ envelope **Knox** Sparkling Gelatine.
1 pint cream, or milk.
2 tablespoonfuls cold water.
Yolks of three eggs.
¼ cup sugar.
1 teaspoonful vanilla.
1½ tablespoonfuls brandy, or
2 tablespoonfuls sherry.

Soak gelatine in cold water five minutes. Make a custard of milk or cream, yolks of eggs and sugar, and add dissolved gelatine; then add flavoring. Let stand in cool place until serving time.

TO MAKE CURRANT, GRAPE OR OTHER JELLY FIRM

If a fruit jelly does not "jell" after being boiled a sufficient length of time, add to each pint a level tablespoonful **Knox** Sparkling Gelatine that has been softened five minutes in one-fourth cup cold water. Heat to the boiling point, skim and strain into the glasses.

IN SOUPS AND GRAVIES

Soups and gravies are much better if gelatine is used in them. By using it in a thin soup stock it will make a rich, nourishing soup.

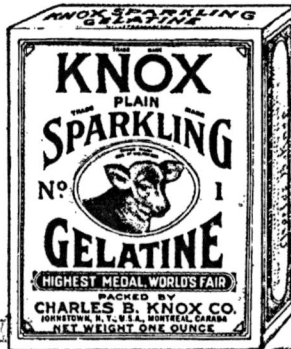

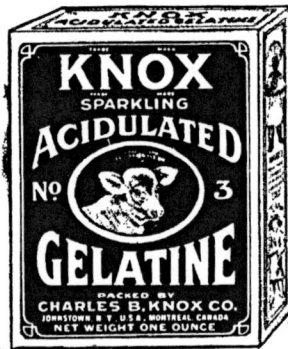

CPSIA information can be obtained at www.ICGtesting.com
Printed in the USA
BVOW012135090112

280172BV00001B/45/A